STUDIES IN MODERN EUROPEAN LITERATURE
AND THOUGHT

General Editor:

ERICH HELLER
Professor of German
in the University College of Swansea

PROUST

Also published in this series

Arturo Barea: UNAMUNO
E. K. Bennett: STEFAN GEORGE
Roy Campbell: LORCA
Hugh F. Garten: GERHART HAUPTMANN
Hans Egon Holthusen: RILKE
P. Mansell Jones: BAUDELAIRE
Martin Jarrett-Kerr: MAURIAC
Janko Lavrin: GONCHAROV
Rob Lyle: MISTRAL
Richard March: KLEIST
Iris Murdoch: SARTRE
L. S. Salzberger: HÖLDERLIN
Elizabeth Sewell: PAUL VALÉRY
Cecil Sprigge: BENEDETTO CROCE
J. P. Stern: ERNST JÜNGER
E. W. F. Tomlin: SIMONE WEIL
Martin Turnell: JACQUES RIVIÈRE
Bernard Wall: MANZONI

Other titles are in preparation

PROUST

BY

J. M. COCKING

BOWES & BOWES
LONDON

First published in 1956 in the Series
Studies in Modern European Literature and Thought
by Bowes & Bowes Publishers Limited, London

Printed in the Netherlands
by Joh. Enschedé en Zonen, Haarlem

CONTENTS

I

Experiments

A la recherche du temps perdu is at once the story of how its hero Marcel came to know his vocation as a novelist and the novel which he wrote as a result. The novel is Proust's; the vocation is a fictional transposition of Proust's. The recent publication of *Jean Santeuil* and *Contre Sainte-Beuve* has provided new evidence of the reality of Proust's vocation; the chapters which follow attempt to sketch that reality, interpret the fiction and explore some of the ways in which they are related.

In 1896 Proust published *Les Plaisirs et les jours*, a collection of short stories, essays and poems, with music by Reynaldo Hahn, illustrations by Madeleine Lemaire and a preface by Anatole France, which was dismissed by most of Proust's friends, and is still dismissed by his critics—apart from its interest as a document on the development of Proust's mind and method—as the work of a dilettante exploiting the more precious tastes of his time. When *A la recherche* began to take its present shape, either in Proust's mind or on paper, is not precisely known. It was assumed, until recently, that he set to work on it seriously between 1904 and 1906, and that between 1896 and the conception of *A la recherche* he did little in the way of writing but translate and comment on Ruskin and fill a number of notebooks with ideas and scraps of conversation for future use.

When André Maurois was preparing his *A la recherche de Marcel Proust*, published in 1949, he was allowed access to these notebooks by Proust's niece, Mme Mante-Proust. He found there early versions of episodes later rewritten for *A la recherche*, and passages apparently intended for a novel written in the third person of which Swann was the hero. Some of these passages concerned events later to be narrated, still in the third person, in *Un amour de Swann*; others were to be transferred from Swann to Marcel and take their place in the self-narrative of *A l'ombre des jeunes filles en fleurs*.

After Maurois had published his book, a research student, Bernard de Fallois, consulted him and was introduced by him to Mme Mante-Proust, who put at his disposal not only those remaining exercise-books which Maurois had not stayed to decipher but some boxes of papers hitherto unexplored since Proust's death. There were found a great quantity of loose sheets of paper, in some cases torn. Fallois put them together to make a kind of novel, and named it *Jean Santeuil* after the principal character, who is obviously the precursor of the Marcel of *A la recherche*—gifted, sensitive and obsessed with the past like him, but unsuccessful, like Swann. Towards the end of 1951 some short passages of this work were published in periodicals, and the whole was issued in three large volumes in 1952. Two years later Fallois presented a further group of hitherto unpublished manuscripts under the title *Contre Sainte-Beuve*. Some of these passages are directly concerned with Sainte-Beuve's critical method; others, though indirectly connected, lead away from Sainte-Beuve to Proust's own affective life, or to the lives of fictional creations like the Guermantes.

The exact dates when Proust began and abandoned these works—the early 'novel' and the study of Sainte-Beuve—are still unknown. But *Jean Santeuil* no doubt bridges the gap between *Les Plaisirs* and the Ruskin translations, and *Contre Sainte-Beuve* appears to have been written in 1908 and 1909, at a time when Proust had already started on his second attempt at a long novel and was uncertain whether his energies were to find expression in a novel or something else. *Les Plaisirs* and *Jean Santeuil* are both feeble compared with *A la recherche*. *Contre Sainte-Beuve* is still the work of an explorer rather than a discoverer. But all these works mutually reflect light which can be caught and concentrated back on to the last. The Proust who wrote the first two was a fundamentally unhappy and frustrated man, and his unhappiness was in some ways very like Baudelaire's, in which Proust himself sensed a close affinity with his own. We may put this down to inherited temperament, as both Baudelaire and Proust were inclined to do, or we may believe with the Existentialists that they chose their suffering. Or we may think that the reality was too complicated to suffer any explanation as simple as either, and complex enough to include something of both. The fact remains that Baudelaire spoke of a 'feeling of loneliness from childhood, the feeling of an eternally lonely destiny', and that Proust, too, felt cut off both by his exaltations and his abasements from the people among whom he lived. Both found their satisfactions and sympathies in works of art; both felt, when they had created their own, that they were showing the reader, who was blind but willing, truths, some of them unwelcome, which it would profit his soul to see. All this partly because the two men were naturally alike, but partly also because Proust, having felt the likeness, was anxious to do, in his own way, as well as Baudelaire had done.

Proust felt not only something of Baudelaire's loneliness, but his sexual obsession and sexual guilt; aggravated, in his case, by the guilt of perversion—though he appears to have convinced himself that Baudelaire, too, was a homosexual. But if Baudelaire could shift some of the responsibility for his moral weakness on to his mother as well as his inherited temperament, Proust never used his mother as a scapegoat. He added another guilt, the suffering his moral spinelessness inflicted on the people who cared for him most; and a terrible fear of what the knowledge of his secret life might add to it.

Like Baudelaire, too, Proust knew moments of escape from responsibility and remorse into a sense of freedom and perfect happiness, felt sometimes in connection with books or music, but also—a most un-Baudelairean sentiment which Proust later

8

found it hard to reconcile with his own philosophy of art—before natural beauty. From the joy of these experiences grew his conviction that he was himself a natural artist.

But he could not easily find a way to actualize in words his sense of artistic 'vision', even to particularize the sense into something specific for his own mind to grasp, something other than a vague if positive elation. His duty seemed to lie in the direction of self-exploration and critical scrutiny of the work of other writers; the discovery of what he had in himself to express, the pursuit in accomplished works of clues as to what to look for and what means might be used to express it. But—as far as his 'vision' was concerned—frustration; and, added to frustration, another guilt—snobbery; and another temptation—that of an all-too-easy social success which, he felt, wasted the time he should have spent in self-scrutiny and atrophied the sensitive inner self at which the scrutiny was directed.

Nor were the consequent strains constantly set in the same pattern, the pulls in the same direction. Proust seems to have been torn between lucidity about his own predicament and the desire to rationalize away the unbearable sense of guilt, torn also between guilt and resentment that fear of remorse should set itself between him and his own kind of sensual paradise: guilt and remorse when he gave way to temptation, resentment and regret when he resisted the temptation of opportunity, frustration when he had no opportunity save in imagination. The perversion itself he ascribed to inherited physiological causes; but he seems to have realized that his illness was, to some extent, a withdrawal from responsibility. He saw how far his weaknesses were the condition of his sensibility, and also how they endangered the will to put his gifts to creative purpose. Yet perhaps some compromise was possible. Perhaps the drama of moral guilt could itself be made into literature. Proust, who always looked high for his models, may have once thought of himself seriously, as he later did half ironically, as another Phèdre; at the age of twenty he wrote the name of Phèdre as his favourite heroine, but, on second thoughts, characteristically substituted Bérénice. Social ambition, too, though it seemed to him to be the enemy of his *real* vocation—the expression of his vision—might yield a harvest; perhaps the observation of people and manners, however far removed from those subjective states which seemed to be the essence of the kind of supernatural experience with which the greatest art should be concerned, could be turned to good, if perhaps comparatively humble, literary account.

But Proust's urge to confess, and to make literary capital out of confession, was held in check by a need for discretion as much personal as aesthetic. There were things Proust wanted to explain, aspects of his intimate struggle which even those closest to him had not been able to understand, of which the understanding must mean from the outside world less condemnation

9

and regret, a more unreserved concession of sympathy. But there were also things which these same people must never suspect.

In *Les Plaisirs et les jours*, confession is transposed into the third person and recounted of fictional characters, the most important of them women; it is limited, and eked out with the experiments of a writer who still has his originality to discover, whose determination to write often forces him to inflate slight conceptions, whose pursuit of originality often gives rise to strained preciosity or flippant ebullience. Yet to the retrospective eye, beneath the camouflage and the superficial cultivation of contemporary literary fashions, Proust's obsessions appear— in *La Mort de Baldassare Silvande, Violante ou la mondanité, La Confession d'une jeune fille, La Fin de la jalousie*: death, and the need to come to terms with it; to learn not to fear it, but also not to desire it as a release from destiny unfulfilled, from the task of discovering in himself the god disguised as a fool which Emerson, in a passage quoted by Proust as an epigraph, had called the soul; sexual temptation and remorse, and the decline, with habit, of both remorse and pleasure; illness and its effect on the mind, turning it in upon its own most intimate life from which health, activity and the pursuit of social pleasures may turn it away; the corrosive effect of these social pleasures on the soul itself, which ought rather to be cultivated in music, meditation, solitude, charity and natural beauty; the crowding in, at moments of discouragement and self-disgust, of poignantly contrasting memories of childhood and maternal cherishing; the contrast between the innocence of the mother-centred childhood Eden and the world in which the serpent (here, in *Violante* and *La Confession*, the part is played, for the heroines into whom Proust has transposed himself, by a young cousin) has hissed its promise of sensual pleasures, never again to be done without but always treacherous, unsatisfying and corrupt; the strength and suddenness of impulse, the weakness of will; the constant procrastination of the effort towards the salvation of settled and calm work; the flight from solitary temptation into the distractions of society and the consequent redoubling of the difficulty of choosing solitary contemplation and the life of the soul; and, over all, the complex of hypocrisies which is felt to be not a part of the true self, with which the true and, somehow, always inviolable self is overlaid.

The stories of *Les Plaisirs*, in so many respects cautionary tales, and tributes to a wisdom their author accepted but could not act on, show also a keen awareness of and interest in the ecstasies of the flesh. Anatole France's reference, in his preface, to a depraved Bernardin de Saint-Pierre and an ingenuous Petronius is to the point, though it could be applied more pointedly to certain passages of *A la recherche*—for in that novel Proust has managed more than once to recount events proper to Petronius with an amorality which is not unlike Bernardin de Saint-Pierre's assumption that the passion he is narrating is natural, innocent, and likely to delight the reader's heart. The encounter between Charlus and Jupien, at the beginning of *Sodome et Gomorrhe*, is grotesque; but into this grotesque passion which leaps up in two middle-aged men Proust has transposed some of the poetry which, for Musset, attended *le lit joyeux de deux jeunes époux*. The Petronius in Proust became steadily less ingenuous. When, like Baudelaire, he had shed moral responsibility and guilt in his writing, the result was often, from a literary point of view, happy; the appearance of an all-pervading humour is one sign of the change of attitude. But complacent nastiness was liberated as well as poetry, indecent slapstick as well as comedy. And, when Proust was creating a world in which the hypocrisy which weighed on him was made universal, he universalized also the assumption that every adolescent and adult, when social constraint can be sloughed off, naturally slips away to gratify his appetite for furtive and mostly artificial sexual pleasure.

Les Plaisirs tells us not only something of what Proust needed to write out of his system but something of his exploration of means. Later he was to discard the kind of confession he is using here, the narrative of temptation, sin and remorse which is his own moral drama transposed into the third person but otherwise close to life. Already he is concerned with other aspects of self-expression: with style, for instance, in its traditional sense —the manner of handling words considered as independent of matter, those constants of a literary mind which appear as characteristics whatever the business on which it is engaged. Like Robert Louis Stevenson, another writer with a burden of experience to be thrown off and an experience of delight to be expressed, but a sporadic and too easily derivative imagination, Proust was learning to 'play the sedulous ape', scrutinizing and feeling his way into other literary skins with a success to which the excellence of his pastiche bears witness.

Proust is also concerned with that crude form of catharsis arrived at through cynicism and a withering contempt for the figures to be met with in the social life which inspired such mixed feelings in him. What we miss, in *Un dîner en ville*, is the humour of *À la recherche* and the willingness to concede that the snobbish and ambitious figures at this dinner-party exhibit anything but the contemptible features of human life. The style is neat but too intentionally corrosive. Yet the effectiveness of this contempt and the neatness of its expression depend on that faculty for separating out the strands of a mood or a state of mind which, developed and matured, produces, in the reader of *À la recherche*, the conviction that Proust's account of mental flux is (within the limits of the kind of mental flux with which it deals) both analytically precise and comprehensive, lucid without sacrifice of shades.

Serious and typical as are the preoccupations which underlie the writing of *Les Plaisirs et les jours*, to move from these finished but fragmentary exercises to the shapeless mass of *Jean Santeuil* is to enter the workshop where the real labour is going ahead. This book is a collection of personal impressions and experiences, of ideas about literature, love and social ambition, of vignettes, caricatures and social situations; all unrelated except that they are felt, thought, observed by Jean Santeuil. This 'novel' has no design, no shape and no climax. To account for its inconclusiveness, perhaps, as well as to satisfy the instinct to put distance between confession and himself, Proust attributes the writing of it to the novelist C. C. dies without leaving a manuscript, but his work is published by the narrator of the prologue and his friend who, when they had met C. on holiday in Brittany, had been given a copy of the work as it then stood.

But C. and Jean Santeuil are as intimately related as the Swann and Marcel of the later book. Jean, it is pointed out, has some of C.'s faults, more good qualities, like sensibility and kindness, and much poorer health. But at this stage it is Jean Santeuil who has suffered most and shown no talent for no particular art, while C. is the successful novelist; later Swann is to be the failure and Marcel is to be gloriously successful.

C. writes in Brittany, and the people he meets there come into his books. But the things and people he writes about (we are told in the prologue) are only the pretexts for the working of his visionary power. The most trivial events can awaken his imagination and liberate his sense of poetry, can become 'these moments of deep illumination when the spirit penetrates to the heart of all things and lights them as the sun can light the depths of the sea'. This idea of artistic vision piercing to the infinite soul of things reminds us of Emerson and Baudelaire; and, just as Baudelaire considered in parallel the ecstasies of imaginative vision and drugs, Proust writes that C.'s joy is one which other men 'seek in poisons only to expiate in suffering'.

C., in fact, has in his make-up more of the typical poet than of the typical novelist. He has, he says, no power of invention; the people he writes about and the situations they find themselves in are those he has come across in his own life. But the narrator, musing on this, is sceptical of its absolute truth. Did C. *really* know all the characters he wrote about? How far did he change the reality of his life to make his books? What are 'the secret relations, the necessary metamorphoses which exist between the writer and his work, reality and art, or rather ... between the appearances of life and the reality itself which permanently underlies life and which art reveals'? Proust is writing here as a would-be Symbolist who has not yet discovered the Way.

And, in the novel itself, Jean Santeuil is presented as a 'subjective idealist'; but he has not yet thoroughly learned the symbolist lesson that, as an apprehension of the 'real', art is more direct and 'truer' than philosophy. Marcel's heroes and spiritual guides are to be the artists Bergotte, Elstir, Vinteuil; Jean Santeuil's hero is his philosophy master, M. Beulier—as Proust's, at the age of twenty, was M. Darlu, who had taught him philosophy at the Lycée Condorcet. Traves, the novelist Jean meets in the story, is a visionary like C. himself; but he does not know it. His overt philosophy is materialistic; M. Beulier could have taught him, as he had taught Jean, that science leads to blind scepticism, that the self is absolute, that God exists. For God, whose absence in *A la recherche* Mauriac has deplored, is named in Jean Santeuil as the sanction of the beauty which is also truth; it was later that Proust exercised his intelligence to the utmost to do without the sanction while keeping the value of the experience.

Here God, as, later, beauty, is revealed only in subjective vision; the outside world (so the theory implies) has no interest except as providing occasions for this. Proust is exhibiting the kind of spiritual onanism which Hegel thundered against, and which so many self-styled Hegelians among the Symbolists, who did not grasp the difference between Hegel and Fichte, exhibited; and he takes it upon himself to correct Stendhal's view of love, to transpose it into his own terms. For, according to Proust, Stendhal is an artist in spite of his philosophy, which like Traves's, is 'materialistic'. Stendhal attaches value to relations between the self and the outside world, and, consequently, to the outside world; this, according to Proust, is a mistake. Of the two brands of romantic Idealism, that which is paralleled by the objective Idealism of Hegel and that which is paralleled by the subjective Idealism of Fichte; of the two kinds of romantic eroticism, that which seeks to express itself in fertility and action, and that which seeks a narcissistic self-possession—Stendhal stands for the first and Proust for the second. Here is the very root of Proust's conception of love, which is to play so great a part in *A la recherche*; and some will judge it to be a piece of sophistry based on a pathologically limited experience. For Stendhal, writes Proust, 'what gives us a love of solitude and a thousand thoughts, what makes nature comprehensible and eloquent . . . is love. We cannot go so far. Love is indeed like poetry in that it frees us from other people, plunges us into solitude and makes us feel the charm of nature. But it is a queer phase of life, this constraint of poetry which debars an individual from every individual concern, this unity of nature reduced to a dual individuality. An individual, however remarkable—and in love the other individual is usually anything but remarkable —has no right to limit our inner life in this way.' There is no relation, Proust affirms, between this 'other' and our own inner life. For Proust the Platonic hermaphrodite has become a Narcissus who projects his own image on to a stranger. The sophistry is the more persuasive in that it contains an observable truth; no doubt the romantic lover projects, but not on to a blank screen. And what he projects is itself not necessarily as narcissistically self-contained as Proust would have us think. Imagination can collaborate with, as well as merely 'use', instinct, at the point of integrity which Proust and his like

13

deny. It is a pity that Proust, with his penetration, and his own kind of integrity, which is intellectual rather than moral, had not a greater range of experience to account for.

If his theory of love, in *Jean Santeuil*, is settling into a form which could shape a number of separate love stories, Proust is obviously having difficulty in applying his transcendental aesthetic to his own case, in putting the theory into practice. C., we are given to assume, does not write about his experiences of divine illumination but about the experiences which are the occasions of the illumination; and the visionary quality is conveyed by the manner of his recounting. But Proust, strong in his philosophical conviction, has an essentially didactic side to him; he longs to get straight to the point, to demonstrate the transcendence, to talk about the visionary moments as such, to explain how they are linked to the rest of his experience—for instance, as we have just seen, to love. And, when he concentrates on the centre of it all, the visionary moments themselves, there is nothing much to talk about. He can only state, in 'elevated' style, that such moments are known to the artist; they seem to be like the similar moments referred to, but not in essence recaptured, in *A la recherche*—the obscure message of the Martinville spires, for instance, and the Balbec trees. Instead of writing poems, like Baudelaire, or novels, like Traves, which *are* the transcendent experiences, Proust can only talk *about* them, and about a life spent in the attempt to discover how to write a novel like Traves's—like Stendhal's—but, perhaps, more purely expressive of the beauty which is also truth. But the sense of beauty, of rising out of the mortal state, does not seem to have arisen often, for Proust, out of the spectacle of human life; rather out of a pattern like the steeples, a glimpse of nature like the trees, and, principally and most vividly, out of the peculiarly abrupt and clear memories to which sensations could stimulate his mind.

The cult of memory, and the connection between memory and the experience of transcendence, of plenitude and freedom, are already firmly established in *Jean Santeuil*. The pleasure of remembering is connected with the pleasure of reading, and carries with it the idea of vocation, of an impulse and even a duty to write. Comparison of the two novels leaves no doubt that Proust's mind was persistently occupied with the problem of explaining a felt correspondence between reading books and remembering his own past, and explaining what, for him, was the peculiar and unlifelike pleasure of both.

There were hints to be found in the literature of the nineteenth century in which he was steeped—the literature which Jean reveres as the revelation of 'mysterious truth' and puts far above the previous century beloved of Traves, who, in this respect also, is like Stendhal. Proust himself mentions, in *Le Temps retrouvé*, instances of affective memory released by sensation in Chateaubriand, Nerval and Baudelaire. Professors Jean

Pommier and Justin O'Brien have considerably lengthened the list. M. Pommier quotes a striking example from Musset's *Confession* of a memory felt as submerged but struggling to rise like a cork held below the water, where the image and the dramatic presentation are very close to Proust's images and style in the narrative of the *madeleine* incident. But the most interesting name on Proust's list is Baudelaire's.

For Baudelaire had said both that genius was the power to recover childhood and that literature was the gateway to heaven. He had exalted memory and writing as means of returning to a lost paradise; and for Proust, as he wrote in *Le Temps retrouvé*, our true paradises are always those we have lost. So when Marcel, after his 'revelation', looks to the romantic literature he knows so well for confirmation of the value of his new 'knowledge', it is to Baudelaire he turns. But he is interrupted—conveniently for him, exasperatingly for the reader—in his meditation. It will be suggested later that Proust never found a satisfactory theory to explain how his own 'vision-through-memory' could be equated with the supernaturalism of the Romantics. But he did find a way of conveying the feelings to which it gave rise and the sense of certain correspondences which eluded intellectual analysis. What *Jean Santeuil* lacks, and *A la recherche* has, is the construction of experience into a philosophical drama, with involuntary memory as the *deus ex machina*. Everything which Proust says about memory in *A la recherche* is explicit or implicit in *Jean Santeuil*; but not surrounded with the mystery of sleep and the unconscious, preceded by presentiments, struggling free of enchantments, suddenly appearing with a preternatural vividness of sensation to raise a past self from the dead. The old grandfather, M. Sandré, lives in a past which, for him, is the true present; and his mind moves to events in the past in a flash. 'The genius of memory which, faster than electricity, goes round the world, and as quickly goes round the world of time, had set him down before he could even tell if a second had passed.' Who does not recognize, in this banality, the thought which, surrounded with the mystery of sleep and coming after a carefully dramatic preparation, was to give the rich suggestiveness of 'A sleeping man has round him in a circle the succession of hours, the order of years and worlds'? M. Sandré triumphs over time through memory, but his triumph looks pale in the light of common day.

The theme of aesthetic decline, for which memory is the only compensation, is clearly stated. But again it is not dramatized, no conclusions are drawn, and much of the novel is quite without relation to it. The beauty of lilacs comes to be felt by *Jean Santeuil* as the beauty of his own childhood; and, in the long section of the novel which describes Jean's summer holidays at Etreuilles Proust is evidently searching his memory for the impressions which lie at the root of his own aesthetic preferences. Apple blossom is more satisfying than the finest flowers in the world because its colours and shapes and textures have in them the feeling of the past in which they were first known. But most of all Jean is moved by pink hawthorn, the essence of spring and centre of many memories, ranging from the decorated altar of the church to the appetite for cream cheese with strawberries crushed in it. The sheer animal pleasure of food and bed, post-prandial torpor and hot water bottles is much more in evidence in *Jean Santeuil* than in *A la recherche*. In the latter, the number of images which take their effect from the simpler sensualities is striking; but their pleasure is carefully worked into contexts more sublime. *Jean Santeuil* shows sensation in the raw state, a crudely functioning imagination and the aspiration to transcendence through literature. The three have still to fuse.

In the last three chapters of the sixth part of *Jean Santeuil* Proust tries to come to grips with the peculiar experience of happiness which memory brings him, and in the last of the three the distinction between memory in the ordinary sense and memory stimulated by renewed sensation at last becomes clear. At Begmeil, in Brittany, Proust writes, Jean felt pleasure at the sight of the sea, but no real sense of its beauty. 'The mind seeks in vain, the eye looks in vain; it seems it is not by them that aesthetic enjoyment can be felt. Can it be felt even by memory? No. Next year Jean tried to remember these drives and describe them, but felt no pleasure.' But if, long afterwards, he goes to stay in Switzerland and drives by the lake of Geneva at a moment when it has a look of the sea, the magic of that past and apparently wasted time is felt at last. 'Between the lake and himself, what is there that was not between the sea and himself, which would not be between the lake and himself if he had not seen the sea in the first place?' Imagination, perhaps, which Proust thinks of as an 'invisible substance' only to be applied to a past recovered; and we are off on a rambling speculation which covers some of the ground of *Le Temps retrouvé* but is a good deal more naïve and more consistently centred on the century's clichés about imagination, conceived as the organ which serves the eternal and gives us glimpses of our spiritual home. The final exhortation, full as it is of the real pathos of Proust's inner life, is comic literature: 'So let us love, let us know all the times of our life, let us be sad in bedrooms, let us not even be too downcast that we have lived in elegant carriages and in drawing-rooms. We do not know on which of the days when we look for beauty in a mountain or a sky we shall find it in the sound of a rubber wheel or the smell of a material . . .' As a view of human happiness this Micawberism of the emotions is limited indeed; Proust was to learn to make better dramatic use of involuntary memory, and to build round his private and eccentric gospel a work of more universal acceptance.

What he had to discover was not so much the metaphysical explanation of his joy in memory as his own power to create. *Jean Santeuil* is preceded by an epigraph. It occurs to the reader that Proust may have intended this as C.'s epigraph for his book, but as now printed it refers to Proust's. 'Can I call this book a novel? It is less perhaps and much more, the very essence of my life collected with no admixture, in those times of agony when it is distilled. This book was never made, it was garnered.' Having been garnered, it had still to be made.

But if Proust, like C., felt he had little power of invention, the narrator's scepticism about the exact relation of C.'s life to his narrative warns us that, already in *Jean Santeuil*, we must expect reality to be adapted. No doubt Proust, like C., wrote 'nothing out what he had personally felt'; no doubt also he wrote about those feelings both as they arose in life and as they in turn gave rise to those crude imaginative constructions which are wishful fantasies.

There is a good deal of wishful fantasy in *Jean Santeuil*. The story of Jean's friendship with Henri de Réveillon bears the stamp of daydream elaborated on a real foundation. Henri de Réveillon is obviously the prototype of Robert de Saint-Loup; Robert is generally considered to have been modelled, at least in his virtues, on Bertrand de Fénelon and his friends, the Duc d'Albuféra and the Duc de Guiche. Henri de Réveillon is, in one chapter of *Jean Santeuil*, referred to as *Bertrand* de Réveillon. But, though the chronology of Proust's life has been uncertainly established by his biographers, it seems unlikely that Proust knew Fénelon at the age when Jean knew Henri. On the other hand Proust did, at that age, stay with friends in the country— at Chantilly, for instance, and at L'Isle-Adam with one Joyant. It seems probable that his imagination was already working up reality into something more satisfying; that, here, it was projecting his aristocratic acquaintances back into less aristocratic acquaintances and building up a situation which he would have liked to find himself in. Henri is the only son of the first Duke of France, and a schoolfriend of Jean's. In temperament he is the opposite of Jean, both active and disciplined, frank and straightforward. He has never known the meaning of snobbery and scorn, writes Proust with significant envy and admiration, never felt the need to hide snobbery or the wish to express scorn. Jean's schoolmaster, a Republican—not, of course, the beloved M. Beulier—persuades Jean's parents that his friendship with Henri is a bad moral influence; which is the opposite of the truth. There is a violent family quarrel, after which Jean manages to repress his feelings of violent hatred for his parents, reminds himself that his mother will not always be with him, and makes it up in a flood of sentimental righteousness. This may well be a true account of one of the family explosions in which Proust was sometimes involved by his pursuit of acquaintances and a way of life outside his class. The friendship with Henri, however, continues; the Duke and Duchess are delighted with Jean; he becomes a second son and stays with them for long periods in the country. The account

17

of these visits to Réveillon in some ways parallels the earlier account of summer holidays spent at Etreuilles; but the 'poetry' it expresses is that of utter privacy, complete liberty and unlimited creature comfort. There are no cousins to hide from, no *real* parents to moralize and harry; none of the drawbacks of family life but all its cosy security. It is, in fact, very much what the naïve young mind assumes the lives of the rich and powerful to be. The ideal parents of this dream-world are the first Duke and his lady, the ideal brother is both complement and friend. There is also a buxom servant who creeps to Jean's bedroom at night. Between them, the Réveillons shepherd Jean through the perils of high society, bolstering his self-assurance and avenging the snubs he suffers.

The account of Jean's entry into society gives some insight, though it must remain conjectural, into the timidities, wounds and frustrations which underlay the easy superficial success of which Proust's biographers make so much. The chronology of his conquest of society remains a little hazy. His biographers divide his life into successive periods without breaking these down into successive details, and indeed in a life consisting chiefly of an alternation of social engagements and secluded privacy it is difficult to do otherwise. From the salon of Mme Straus, mother of his schoolfriend Jacques Bizet, widow of the composer of *L'Arlésienne* and daughter of Halévy who composed *La Juive*, Proust moved on to the salons of Mme Aubernon, Mme Gaston de Caillavet, Mme Loynes, and perhaps to those, more socially distinguished, of the Comtesse Greffulhe and the Baronne Aimery de Pierrebourg. He met the Comtesse d'Haussonville, the Princesse de Wagram, the Princesse Mathilde. In 1893 began his curious relationship with the Comte Robert de Montesquiou-Fezensac, compounded of genuine regard and a sycophancy which could suddenly turn to respectful firmness when Montesquiou shared the anti-Semitism of most of his kind at the time of the Dreyfus affair.

In friendships with people of his own generation he added, to his middle-class schoolfriends of the Lycée Condorcet, the Duc de Guiche, Antoine and Emmanuel Bibesco, the Duc d'Albuféra and the Comte de Salignac-Fénelon. But if, as Derrick Leon wrote, 'by the time Proust was twenty-five, he had penetrated into almost every stratum of the social sphere', he was still, in two senses, an outsider. He was a learner longing to be assimilated, and he was an observer fascinated by observation for its own sake. *Jean Santeuil* suggests that Proust never forgave the Faubourg Saint-Germain for the slights and humiliations attending a social progress which itself troubled his conscience, and never forgave even the friendliest of his most aristocratic acquaintances for the distance by which they fell short of the Duke and Duchess of his first dream. For the closest friends of his own age he seems to have had a genuine feeling of warmth, and the feeling glows in his portrait of Robert de Saint-Loup.

But Proust could no more be assimilated into their world of values and habits than he could be assimilated into that of his own family; of the two environments, both incompatible with himself, he fell back on the more familiar. In so far as he concerned himself at all with moral judgments, he came to put the virtues of his own family, 'les vertus de Combray', above the virtues of the Faubourg, and retreated to the conviction that he carried, within himself, values superior to both.

But until he reached this position, and broke with both worlds after the death of his parents, Proust was no doubt divided, in his curiosity about genealogy, protocol and convention, between the detachment of the zoologist and the desire to perform faithfully the carefully regulated movements he was observing. He questioned the old Comtesse de Beaulaincourt about the manners and customs of the past, and Prince Antoine Bibesco about precedence, relationships and titles. He gently reproached his mother for addressing a letter to 'Fénélon' with a superfluous acute accent and spelling Bibesco's name with a 'k'.

In his social ambition he had, like Balzac's climbers, a model; his was Charles Haas. Haas, the Jewish stockbroker's son, appeared to be thoroughly at home in high society; he was a member of the Jockey Club and a friend of the Prince of Wales. When Proust found that he could not achieve the satisfaction which he imagined success had brought to Haas, but saw how to achieve his own in another way, he made Swann out of what he knew of Haas, what he remembered of his former self, and perhaps the culture and learning of Charles Ephrussi, founder of the *Gazette des beaux arts*, and something of the character and mannerisms of his own Jewish uncle, Louis Weil. Swann is a social success and an artistic failure; Marcel renounces social success, becomes a creative artist, and cruelly satirizes the denizens of the social zoo.

If, in *Jean Santeuil*, the dream of the happiness to which social success was to open the door is still intact, however crudely expressed by Jean's relations with the Réveillons, the bitter satire occasioned by the impact of hard reality has already begun. Though Jean enjoys the full sunshine of the Réveillons's affection and esteem, when he begins to make his way in the Paris salons he is blinked at by lesser lights and snubbed. Being more sensitive than vain, writes Proust, he feels hurt rather than resentful; yet somehow Providence, in the persons of the Duke and Duchess, manages to avenge his hurt and inflict more than compensating wounds on the unfortunate women who have offended him. The chapters in which this pattern is worked out can scarcely have been intended as consecutive; it looks rather as though Proust, finding a special attraction in the theme, had worked over it several times to try out the effect. As the passages are now printed, the effect is one of obsession with the sweetness of revenge, disguised as providential justice. To measure Proust's progress as an artist, we have only to compare these narratives to the scene in *La Prisonnière* where Charles, humiliated and shattered by the outburst of revolt which Mme Verdurin has inspired Morel to utter, is protected and reinstated by the sympathy and regard of the Queen of Naples, who gives him her arm and bears him proudly off with words of contempt for the *canaille* among which they find themselves. The emotions are the same; but now Proust has invented a situation in which the reader is prepared to share them.

In *Jean Santeuil*, invention on the narrative level scarcely rises above wishful fantasy. But the subjective preoccupation in no way inhibits Proust's strikingly shrewd observation of manners; and he is already taking another kind of revenge in caricature. The Réveillons are idealized figures and exempt from satirical comment, but every formula and gesture through which the Duke expresses one or other shade of aloof politenesss is catalogued like the habits of an animal in a natural history. Mme Marmet, the third-rate, snobbish, ambitious and vulgar hostess who more than once hurts Jean's feelings and is as often confounded, is cruelly and contemptuously portrayed and treated. So is M. Guéraud-Houppin, an uncle by marriage who pretends, at a reception, not to have heard of his nephew until Jean's arrival, in the company of the Duchess, plunges him in an agony of embarrassment. More gratuitously cruel is the portrait of Henri de Réveillon's aunt, an inoffensive old maid whose only crimes are literary snobbery combined with utter ignorance and her pride in a vague acquaintance with Sully-Prudhomme. These sketches are amusing as well as cruel, and the savagery would be less perturbing if it were not camouflaged behind the 'beautiful, thoughtful eyes' and the sensitive, well-meaning nature of Jean Santeuil himself.

Personal impressions, impressions of reading, the tendency to live in the past, the experience of revelation through memory, the invention of social situations, observation of manners, caricature, the psychology of sexual passion and snobbery—all these are to be found already in *Jean Santeuil*. In spite of the epigraph and C.'s remark that he has no powers of invention, some degree of invention there undoubtedly is. But the elements of the book are not correlated. The last chapters speak of the ageing of Jean's parents and play on the theme of time and flux, and there the book simply peters out.

Proust is casting about for his own material and manner, and testing his own powers against a number of models. His literary ambitions seem to have canalized themselves into three tendencies, and as he explores each there are echoes from his models amounting to pastiche. The first and most central of these three tendencies is the 'mystical', drawing its nourishment from the idealism of romantic literature from Rousseau to the Symbolists, and philosophy from Kant to Bergson. The second is the ambition, centred on Balzac and Saint-Simon, to write the sociological history of a period in terms of personalities and, closely related to this, the ambition of a pure psychological analyst, a student of the general characters of human behaviour, centred on La Bruyère and the great moralists, and stimulated by the positivism of Proust's own century and the prestige of science. *Contre Sainte-Beuve* confirms our sense of Proust's uncertainty about the line he should follow, and some of the notes quoted in Fallois's preface show that Proust was at once genuinely at a loss and inclined to blame himself for irresolution. The decline of spontaneous lyrical feeling in himself led him to think he must give up the Romantic vision in favour of observation and analysis: to a landscape which no longer moved him, he wrote: 'You have nothing more to say to me; it is people who interest me now'. Yet when he read Sainte-Beuve, the transcendental idealism in himself was fanned to a flame of revolt against Saint-Beuve's systematic confusion between the artist and the man, and went on burning on its own with a fresh creative light. Proust was, at this stage, swinging between feeling and analysis. The problem set by his manifold gifts and interests was that of finding an artistic unity for the material they provided, of bringing feeling and analysis together in a single conception.

II

Reference-Points

Over a quarter of a century ago Ernst-Robert Curtius wrote that Proust's style is an intricate combination of intellectualism and impressionism, of rigorous logical analysis and the recording of the finest shades of sensation and feeling; these two modes of experience, he suggested, were inseparable in Proust's mind. Many critics since then have puzzled and fought with each other over the way in which these two modes are related, and Bergson's name has figured largely in the discussion. There is no doubt that to compare Proust with Bergson is to arrive at a better understanding of both, but too much attention to the comparison has sometimes obscured Proust and his novel behind a fog of philosophical polemic. At one extreme Fiser assumes that Bergson said the last word about art and that Proust is the supreme example of a Bergsonian artist; at the other, Benda sees Bergson's philosophy as pernicious and proclaims that Proust is a great novelist because his work shows the traditional virtues of the novel, observation and the capacity to analyse the structure and motivation of the behaviour narrated. Such extreme views often imply a distressingly over-simplified idea of what Bergson said art ought to be and of what art, in fact, is; of what Proust said about his novel and of what the novel, in fact, turned out to be.

The mind which sees Bergson as *a* revelation but not *the* Revelation, which sees Proust as *an* artist but not *the* Artist, will approach their relationship differently from critics like Fiser;

will see them as two major intellectual phenomena obviously related, yet as obviously distinct. Related first by their historical situation; and, in this respect, not only to each other but to a host of others. To Ruskin, first; we have studies of Proust's affinity with Bergson, of Proust's with Ruskin, of Bergson's with Ruskin. Still to be studied in detail is Proust's affinity with Emerson, quotations from whom appear as epigraphs to parts of Proust's first book, *Les Plaisirs et les jours*. There is the transcendental idealism which unites Emerson to Carlyle and Ruskin, and all three to the French Symbolists, and all these to Proust. But turn the leaves of Emerson's essays and you will come across many correspondences with Proust more particular than the conception of life as symbolizing a dimension outside life; for instance this:

> When the act of reflection takes place in the mind, when we look at ourselves in the light of thought, we discover that our life is embosomed in beauty. Behind us, as we go, all things assume pleasing forms, as clouds do far off. Not only things familiar and stale, but even the tragic and terrible are comely, as they take their place in the pictures of memory... In these hours the mind seems so great, that nothing can be taken from us that seems much. All loss, all pain is particular: the universe remains to the heart unhurt ... For it is only the finite that has wrought and suffered; the infinite lies stretched in smiling repose.

With the word 'involuntary' added to memory, with the 'act of reflection' suitably defined, and with some adjustment of the style, this passage could take its place in any one of a dozen contexts in *A la recherche du temps perdu*. Yet one remains convinced that when Proust read passages like this in Emerson, he was reading of states of mind which were already familiar or, at most, feeling his familiar states pulled into a particular focus and invested with a particular significance. This does not mean that Proust, when he came to fix his own focus and suggest his own significance, would not return, by way of reference, to Emerson's. Influences of this kind play their part in the formation of a sensibility, if only by reinforcing tendencies already present or bringing out the latent. But they are diffuse and overlapped with others, and if Proust's sensibility was to some extent modified by prose like Emerson's, the ideas which Emerson's prose implied had to run the gauntlet of Proust's intelligent scrutiny and be modified in turn, as far as was necessary for them to fit Proust's philosophical and artistic scheme.

What overlap is there in Bergson and Emerson? To state what common ground they might appear to Proust to occupy is to recognize how, in the matter of such affinities, intellectual rigour gives way to feeling, and metaphysical propositions to the *sensibility* of transcendence. Proust, metaphysically baulked eventually made his clearest statement of his central proposition in an inconclusive form: 'One's real life is elsewhere, not in life so-called, nor yet in what we think of as the after-life, but in some dimension *outside* life, if a word that draws its meaning from the conceptions imposed on us by space can be said to have any meaning in a world freed from spatial disciplines . . .' This is intellectually vague enough to accord with both Bergson and Emerson; yet in their interpretations of the 'otherness' of the 'real' life, the life of the spirit, Bergson and Emerson diverge. For both, 'real' life is life when it is properly known; and the proper knowledge of life primarily depends not upon reason but upon a faculty whose operations the untimely intrusion of reason is likely to hinder. But Bergson's 'otherness' is immanent and Emerson's is transcendent; and if, on that issue, Proust never made up his mind, he took refuge in thinking and valuing as if the ideas for which he felt devotion were, in some way, transcendent.

Baudelaire, when he found his mind could encompass no system adequate to the complexity of his experience and the strength of his intuitive conviction and values, took refuge, as he wrote himself two years before the publication of *Les Fleurs du mal*, in 'l'impeccable naïveté'; in the untutored vision of the artist, in the poetic expression of his intuitive values as their only pure expression and, consequently, for him, the only final truth. Proust was less willing than Baudelaire to take refuge in 'l'impeccable naïveté'. He might have been content to do so if his own naïve genius could have produced Baudelaire's results; but like other successors of Baudelaire he found that the sympathy of his feeling with Baudelaire and the transcendental tradition was, in itself, artistically sterile. As far as we know Proust never made the mistake of thinking himself a poet, unless in those verses included in *Les Plaisirs* which might be taken as a feeble attempt to exploit the vein of Baudelaire's 'Les Phares'. The poetry of which he was capable went eventually to nourish his prose, but only when 'naïveté' in Baudelaire's and the more current sense had been supplemented by sophistication. Proust's intellectual curiosity was as persistent as his aesthetic sensibility was delicate, and the speculations of his intelligence were not, as Baudelaire's, carried on outside the work of art but as part of its very substance. The coherence of *A la recherche* is planned and established by the intelligence.

Yet the coherence is not itself purely intellectual, not philosophical, for the materials which Proust's planning intelligence had to deal with had been secreted naturally and without premeditation by his temperament in a hard and, at first, quite unsuccessful struggle to come to terms with life. The hardness of that struggle opened Proust's sympathy to much of the pessimism of the century in which his mind was rooted; to Hardy's, for instance, to the very sense of fatality that Bergson strove against, in which time is the leading agent, and scientific determinism the principal mental component.

Mention of this sense of fatality reminds us of the precariousness of defining and attributing paternity to literary influence. The pessimism centred on time, on the cyclical view of history, on the insignificance of the individual span in the aeons—this pessimism is part of the spirit of the age. Proust's obsession with time has been attributed to the influence of his philosophy master, Darlu, of Bergson, of Ruskin, of George Eliot, as well as of Hardy. But he lived in a century whose poetry begins, in the anthologies, with *Le Lac*, and abounds in references to the relentlessness of clocks, a century divided between historicism and escape into eternities which sometimes appear synthetic, between the majority outlook of confidence in progress and ultimate happiness and the minority refusal of the values of life in favour of art. Bergson's philosophy was an attempt to resolve these dichotomies, in terms of which Proust, meditating on his own predicament, could respond to some but not all. For the rest he was very much a man of the century to which Bergson strove to point out the errors of its ways.

So, whenever we set about estimating an influence, or even an affinity, we must keep our eye on the background. If we fix our eyes only on the pair of minds we are considering, and conscientiously tabulate every parallel idea, feeling, value and belief, we shall find, when our glance is lifted, that a good many items appear to need to be struck out as property common to more than our pair. Even in these cases, one particular formulation of a generally held idea, one particular expression of a widespread feeling may prove to have attracted particular attention; and then it may be illuminating to discover why. But it is equally illuminating to discover why what is *not* assimilated has been rejected.

This is the case with Bergson and Proust. Related first by their historical situation, which relates them both with many others, they are seen to be related in a closer way, by parallel observations of detail and even parallel images. There seems now to be little doubt that Proust borrowed ideas, sometimes slightly transposed, from Bergson, and even borrowed, with transposition as slight, Bergson's means of expression. But to move from this observation to the conclusion that the novel is to be interpreted and assessed in Bergsonian terms is hazardous; Bergson's ideas were by no means the only ones Proust found it convenient to adapt to his own purpose, not even, perhaps, the most fruitful. The evidence now available suggests that what there is of Bergsonian optimism in *A la recherche* is superimposed on a pessimistic ground, or on a ground in which pessimism about life is complementary to optimism about art, in which art, or the 'ideas' which art expresses, is the only intimation of a transcendent and entirely satisfactory state of being. Bergson's contribution to Proust's *summa* could only be accepted when Bergson's sense of the meaningfulness of life was matched by Proust's clear notion of his own purpose and the way to set

about it, and even then much of what Bergson had to say was
stubbornly rejected. To interpret Proust's novel, we must look
at the novel and at Proust. We must bear in mind every influence we can discover, but keep our eye on the receiving end.
And then we shall discover that, if Proust has had no imitators,
it is not only because he was so original; it is also because he
sucked so much nourishment into his own great plant that his
successors had to grow roots in other ground. Few minds have
been more generously nourished than Proust's upon the substance of other minds.

And we shall do well to bear in mind Curtius's terms: intellectualism and impressionism, analysis and sensibility, rejecting the over-simple views of those who would persuade us
that the impressionism is all part of the analysis, or the intellectualism an unavoidable aberration from the impressionistic
ideal (a view which Proust himself was too ready to foster);
we must defend ourselves from the temptation to describe the
work in terms of what an ideal work ought to be, and provisionally
at least, turn a sceptical eye on programmes; even Bergson's;
even Proust's. The study of a century and a half of romantic
programmes suggests that the complexity and subtlety of artistic
achievements are often more than doctrine can encompass, and
raise more questions than theory can answer. But there is little
doubt that Proust studied both the programmes and achievements
of writers who caught his imagination, and that they were many.

During the years when Proust's still blurred conception of
his novel was hovering between a poetical expression of intimate
spiritual states and a more objective treatment of the passions
of social ambition and love, moving on (as we shall see) to
contain the latter while keeping its centre of gravity near the
former, his literary culture seems to have developed in a corresponding way. Jean Santeuil and Marcel, like Proust and his
schoolfriends, become period-conscious, modernity-conscious,
first of all in terms of loyalty to the poetry of the Parnasse;
Leconte de Lisle was still in the ascendant, while Symbolism,
as a movement, was still in its heroic period. But all three loved
books, and enjoyed the intimate delight of reading, before they
were caught up in the collective and more dubious exaltation
of being up-to-date and snobbish about the past. Jean Santeuil
learned a good deal of Musset and Hugo by heart before the
literary snobs converted him to Verlaine and Leconte de Lisle
and taught him to feel contempt for the Romantics; Marcel,
willing at first to listen seriously to Bloch's statement that Racine
and Musset had managed to write one good line each which
fulfilled Leconte de Lisle's requirements, later restored Racine
and Musset to his literary pantheon and scourged the Blochs of
this world with both mockery and argument. He had accepted
the truth of a lesson which Baudelaire had taught; that beauty
is eternal but that the way of perceiving beauty and the forms
of its expression must continually change. He studied the new

ways and forms of his time in Symbolism and Impressionism, and allowed Impressionism, in particular, to open his sensibility to the spectacle of contemporary life; but he also looked for the beauty reflected in the different sensibilities of other ages. His taste moved forward with the present but also enveloped more and more of the past.

And steadily, in his culture, the classical writers—to whose work Jean Santeuil was, at first, indifferent—came into their own. Racine, like the Renaissance painters, is a little too marked by the pomps and affectations of a splendid era not to contrast humorously with Proust's sometimes mischievous (and limited) sense of reality. If, at twenty, he had sometimes cast himself for the role of Phèdre, his production of himself in that role never went beyond the creation of the tempted and fallen young women of *Les Plaisirs*. As we saw earlier, on second thoughts his favourite heroine was Bérénice—not the most typical of Racine. His sense of sin shifted from sexual guilt to procrastination; his favourite literary hero, at twenty, was Hamlet. The procrastination ended, the Phèdre theme (as we shall see) was introduced into *A la recherche*, but ironically. The repressed guilt and its attendant feelings which, perhaps, superficially, Proust had outlived, spent its deeply accumulated forces in projecting the circumstances of its original formation into an imagined world, in which they were shown to be normal and as cosmically innocent as Leconte de Lisle's rapacious shark. And otherwise Racine is quoted in contexts where the prestige of his verse clashes amusingly with the trivial incident which brings it to Proust's mind; as when Françoise's emotions about Eulalie are likened to Joas's when he proclaims, with Athalie in mind, that 'Le bonheur des méchants comme un torrent s'écoule'.

Fascinated as he was by aristocracy, Proust paid more attention to the moralists and memorialists of the seventeenth century than to its drama; most particularly dear to him were La Bruyère and Saint-Simon. Apt always to assess life and literature in terms suggested by his own emotional predicament, his preferences embraced the lyrical and the cruelly if finely positive.

If, in the adolescent Proust, Leconte de Lisle—called, in *Jean Santeuil*, 'the last of the Romantics'—flattered both the cult of art and the enjoyment of disillusion, as Proust matured both pleasures were refined. Both became more intellectually fastidious, more subtly interfused with irony and humour. There is a comparable development of sensibility in certain Symbolists—in Laforgue and Corbière, for instance. But in no other writer, certainly no prose writer, do we find quite the same knitting together of strands which nevertheless remain distinguishable, the quite so happy coexistence in one mind of the double vision—the vision of a man accustomed to perceiving the sensuous beauty of the world through the imagination of a great century of poetry, and the vision of a classical observer of mankind who has lived on into a century of scientific determinism.

But Proust was out to write a novel; his problem was to steer, between poetry and satirical observation of manners, a course proper to the novel. And he knew his novelists as well as his poets and moralists. 'The proper understanding of Proust's social world', wrote Ramon Fernandez, 'begins with the observation that in *Le Temps perdu* are to be found the traces and filiations of nearly all the great novels of the nineteenth century'. Just as the story of Jean Santeuil's first adult love affair with Françoise, otherwise called Mme S., is introduced by a discourse on the nature of love, in which Proust is quite obviously setting out to translate Stendhal's theory of crystallization into the terms of his own 'subjective idealism', the story of Jean's friendship with Henri de Réveillon is introduced by a psychology of snobbery where the literary association is with Balzac. Proust does not mention Julien Sorel here, but there is a parallel in his mind between the *arrivisme* of Jean Santeuil (and himself) and that of Rastignac and Rubempré. The narrative of the social rise of Antoine Desroches, a painter who marries Jean's cousin, begins like a pastiche of a Balzac novel and illustrates its philosophy of the contemporary form of social ambition with parallels from *Le Père Goriot*. But the Desroches soon disappear from the scene and play an episodic role.

There seems little doubt, too, that Flaubert offered Proust points of reference for the diagnosis of his own predicament and the construction of his own destiny. It must have occurred to Proust that he was related to a younger and immature self much as Flaubert was related to Mme Bovary. Emma's 'days of reading' in her adolescence at the convent are as important in her destiny as Jean's and Marcel's in theirs, and her tragedy is shown to be due to her spiritual obtuseness before a problem which Flaubert and Marcel saw as the central problem of the artist and believed themselves to have solved. She confuses literature and life, the exaltations of the spirit with the ecstasies of the flesh. We shall have to return to her later, and ourselves make use of her as a reference-point to clarify Proust's ideas.

For Fromentin Proust must have felt both sympathy and antipathy. Dominique, with gifts and problems of temperament not unlike Marcel's, takes what Proust, in his moral incapacity, must have felt to be an abysmally philistine course, rejecting the riches of his sensibility for the well-ordered but morose and half-frustrated life of a gentleman farmer. *Dominique* is indeed far less exhilarating than *A la recherche*; it stands for the more dismal renunciation effected not as the joyful choice of a greater good but as the repression of a feared indiscipline. If Marcel never quite grows up into an adult world, he at least finds his own issue from the dullness of middle age. But if, in reading *A la recherche*, one is rarely reminded of Fromentin except when he is mentioned by name, as he is once or twice as painter and author of *Les Maîtres d'autrefois*, and when, in Proust's pastiche of the Goncourt diary, it is revealed that Mme Verdurin is

27

none other than the Madeleine of Fromentin's novel, there are passages in *Jean Santeuil* which directly recall *Dominique*. Both boys, writing essays for their tutor or schoolmaster, read their own emotions into the historical situations they are writing about. Dominique writes tenderly about Hannibal's defeat because he is about to leave home to go to school; Jean identifies himself with Joan of Arc. Dominique, like Jean and Marcel, is emotionally dependent on sense impressions and has a memory which retains sense impressions more easily than facts. The seasonal and atmospheric impressions of his boyhood home are recorded with remarkable sensuous vividness.

Proust's work, then, is firmly rooted in the French literary tradition. But it is not merely literary. It is rooted in his personal experience. We have seen that Stendhal was absorbed and transmuted. And Fernandez, after noting that all the themes of the century's novels are picked up again in *A la recherche*, goes on to say: 'If these traces are not always recognizable (except to a few initiates) it is because Proust's intelligence, sensibility and imagination have submitted these traces, these elements, to greater pressures, like the high temperatures or chemical agents which distort certain metals. One must always bear these great themes of the novel in mind, and then one realizes what they could become in certain specific psychological conditions.' What, for Proust, built up these imaginative temperatures, precipitated these chemical agents? We have said that his work is not merely literary; it is rooted in his own experience; but if we ask where he found the tools to shape other men's writing to his own imaginative needs, we must answer that it was in other regions of literature. He found his tools in one literature, refined and improved them, and used them to adapt another literature to the purposes proposed by his own experience. Proust's work is not *merely* literary; but it is predominantly so.

He wrote to a friend in 1909 or 1910: 'It is curious that in all the different *genres*, from George Eliot to Hardy, from Stevenson to Emerson, there is no literature which has as much hold on me as English and American literature. Germany, Italy, very often France, leave me indifferent. But two pages of *The Mill on the Floss* reduce me to tears. I know that Ruskin loathed that novel, but I reconcile all these hostile gods in the Pantheon of my admiration.'

The most interesting names in that list are those of George Eliot and Ruskin. For *Jean Santeuil* confirms what L. A. Bisson had already more than half suggested; that George Eliot played as large a part in helping Proust to self-awareness as any philosopher. Her work encouraged him to clear his mind about the 'specific psychological conditions' within which, for example, Balzac's social climbers, Stendhal's lovers, Flaubert's romantic dreamers became distorted, and in their common distortion united, into the Proustian world.

As for Ruskin, another penetrating remark made by

Fernandez, writing of Proust's style, will help us to see what he gave to Proust: 'Slowly and harmoniously Proust's sentences tend to poeticize the real *without transforming it*, the imagination working up every scrap of sensation which the real provides. The precision of the impressionistic notations is, as it were, the security for the graceful or piquant vagaries of the imagination.' The tendency to poeticize the real without transforming it is eminently French; but Proust seems to have learned his impressionistic precision from Ruskin. And from Ruskin he derived a lesson complementary to the one he learned from George Eliot. She helped him to the notion of an imaginative capital laid up in childhood, providing in later life diminishing means which only memory could subsidize; from Ruskin's thought and Ruskin's prose Proust forged an instrument whereby he could reinject imagination into a dreary world.

Of all the correspondences with his own sensibility which Proust must have found in *The Mill on the Floss*, the chief can be summed up in a theme to which George Eliot more than once returns: 'Childhood impressions are the mother-tongue of imagination.' This theme is paralleled in *Jean Santeuil*: 'They say that as we grow older our sensations grow weaker; perhaps, but they are accompanied by the echo of former sensations, like those ageing primadonnas whose failing voice is supported by an invisible choir.' George Eliot prefers an elderberry bush to the finest fuchsia because of the memories it stirs; Proust is moved by may blossom for the same reason. But when we compare the formlessness of *Jean Santeuil* with the design of *A la recherche*, we notice that the coherence of the latter is in great part due to the fact that not only Marcel's love of may blossom but every aspiration of his life is referred back to the patterns which his imagination began to assume in childhood, influenced by natural beauty but also, and even more—which is characteristic of Proust—by the books with which he spent the most delightful part of his life. Proust tried to turn George Eliot's idea into a system, basing upon it the account of a fictional life in which romantic love and social ambition are seen as the pursuit of a poetry already and more fully known in the past.

But, in the later novel, this account of an emotional decline takes its place in a more complex emotional pattern. The falling rhythm of the loss of childhood impressions is counterpointed by the rising rhythm of the growing sense of vocation; the loss of imaginative spontaneity is counterbalanced by a gain of imaginative insight, culminating in the 'revelation' provided by involuntary memory. This final upward swing is foreshadowed in a recurring local pattern: imagination clashes with reality and disintegrates; then, usually under the guidance of an artist, it reawakens in forms compatible with reality. For instance, Marcel goes to Balbec with his head full of the romance of Gothic churches and primitive seas; he is disappointed in the church, until Elstir teaches him to read in its fabric the very spirit of the age which created it; he shades his eyes from the unprimitive yachts and bathers until Elstir teaches him to find beauty in images of contemporary life. No doubt these upward movements, which more than compensate for romantic disillusion by cultivated insight, reflect similar movements in Proust's sensibility between *Jean Santeuil* and *A la recherche*; in life, the man who did most to stimulate them was Ruskin.

Ruskin preached an idealism like Emerson's, but it was an *applied* idealism. He showed Proust exactly how certain works of art could be said to reflect the inner and transcendent life. Proust turned from *Jean Santeuil* to the study and translation of Ruskin because, as he wrote, he sometimes felt that he was piling up ruins, like Casaubon in *Middlemarch*. Ruskin taught him how to set about a real building. He showed him how familiar things become strangely interesting when they are resolved into their complex details, and provided the example of a style in which such details are precisely noted. He suggested a way of according to the dull world of natural experience a prestige reflected from the more satisfactory and exciting world of art, or of viewing the world with a humorous sense of its contrast with a world of art which some of its features recall.

Ruskin's influence is reflected in Proust's minute account of Aunt Léonie's dried lime-flowers, of the rise and change of feeling, of motives, of how milk looks as it comes to the boil. And there is to be noted in both writers a sense of the enduring combined with the evanescent, of the perspective of history and the precariousness of the moment. Ruskin sought a particular fall of sunlight on a building made solidly meaningful by the stretch of its history; at the climax of *A la recherche*, after watching the different momentary lights falling on different aspects of people's characters, we see them solid, and, it seems, fixed at last with the depth of their past behind them.

III

The Plan

In 1906 or thereabouts, Proust had come to a number of interesting but unrelated conclusions about life as experienced by himself; and he had a message, which was that 'real life is in some dimension outside life'. In the literature of the century he had come across this same message in many forms, and in Symbolism particularly he saw an aesthetic ambition directed towards the expression of the experience of this ideal dimension to the exclusion of those of everyday. He had explored philosophy, and found a number of ideas which corresponded with his own intuitions, but he had found no system which could comprehend and account for all his own intuitions, and had been unable to invent one for himself. And so he set about inventing a world in which all that he believed himself to know about human experience could be exemplified, and from which everything of human experience which was irrelevant to his own discoveries and opaque to his understanding would be omitted. In a sense every novelist does this; but few, if any, novelists have done it with the same clarity of intention and the same cerebral method as Proust's. In what E. M. Forster calls novels of prophecy—*Moby Dick* for instance—the novelist, we imagine, is at least in part discovering his purpose as he goes. Not so Proust. He had amassed a number of observations of detail; he was convinced of one 'truth' which was a matter of his own feeling that there was no happiness for him outside himself, no happiness the world could give him other than what he himself had contributed to the world through his own spiritual spontaneity. Baulked of coherence of a purely philosophical order, he interrelated his materials in every possible way, weaving in thread after thread so that each appeared to be related to the others by an internal necessity. In part the plan was determined by the material, by the need to present and justify certain modes of experience valued in a certain way; but the internal necessity of the plan in turn affected the material—its selection, its ordering, its transmuting—and gave rise to the invention of new material. Proust wrote that his book was part memoirs and part novel, and it is in this respect that it left the domain of memoir behind and entered the realm of the novel proper. He invented events, characters, landscapes, artists, works of art to carry patterns of feeling which were felt in that particular way and perceived as or arranged in patterns only at the time of writing the novel. If *Jean Santeuil* seems to be a mixture of tentative and puzzled reporting of actual experience with wishful fantasy, in *A la recherche* the two have fused into an imagined world dominated and ordered by the mind of Proust, where the groping and uncertainty of the young Marcel are always seen against the background of his later conviction and certainty; every apparently shapeless fragment is ready to click into place at the touch of the appropriate spring; the mechanisms are all prepared, and in *Le Temps retrouvé* the sections consisting of groups of fragments were all to fit together into the final pattern. The book represents the creation of a destiny. In the event the final fit is not exact; there are rifts in the mental fabric of Proust's novel. And the individual destiny there portrayed has to be adapted by the reader to provide a conception of the destiny of humanity as a whole. But one has to press to find the cracks, for they are effectively papered over. The rifts are philosophical; they are papered over by the cunning devices of the novelist.

'Man's vices', wrote Baudelaire, 'contain the proof . . . of his inclination towards the infinite . . . In this depravation of the sense of the infinite, in my view, lies the reason for all culpable excesses . . .' Proust, in retrospect, saw his final success as an artist—and at the root of his notion of the artist lies the romantic-symbolist ambition to make the infinite perceptible, to move out of time to eternity—as a precarious victory over the forces of two 'culpable excesses', eroticism and snobbery. He lived first in a state of conflict between these and the attempt to write; the conflict was resolved, and the spiritual calm, content and purposeful assurance reflected in *A la recherche* were made possible when the experience garnered from sexual passion and social ambition was made the very stuff of the book itself, the springboard from which Marcel, like Banville's clown, was to leap into the infinite. By 1906 Proust could feel that he had renounced the world, if not the flesh. He could look out from his ark on the society he had abandoned, about to be engulfed by the rising tide of democracy, with, superficially, the tolerance born of assurance, of confidence in his own kind of superiority. Writing, he behaved towards the aristocrats of his created world as he had seen some of the real aristocrats behave towards himself, with the apparent humility of those who are entirely sure of themselves. But he also avenged his earlier, humiliated self, and appropriated the naked arrogance of some of his creations for his own—and his readers'—satisfaction. In his Balzacian psychology of social ambition in *Jean Santeuil*, Proust remarked: 'Either because his perspicacity takes pleasure in cruelly punishing in other people the shame of feeling these effects (of snobbery) within himself, or rather because writing of his morbid passion even to stigmatize it is another way of cultivating and satisfying it, the novelist who is also a snob will become the novelist who treats of snobs.' These observations are true of Proust himself, and no less in 1906 than in 1896; valid also is his principle that the artist who is the victim of a passion will rationalize his predicament and pretend that he has chosen the way of life to which his passion has condemned him. What has changed is the reason given for the extended study of high society and snobbery. Marcel's social ambition is to be shown as a mistaken pursuit of poetry, an idealist's mirage imaging more substantial spiritual states to be traced back to childhood and Combray; it is in other characters like Legrandin and Mme Verdurin that snobbery appears as a crude and selfish vice, the shamefully unspiritual character of which is imaged in Legrandin's quivering buttocks.

Sexual desire and social ambition Proust felt to be, or rationalized into, the pursuit of something spiritually valued, in the purest sense loved. Romantic love is involved in both; in one case rooted in a subsoil of pure sensuality but rising into successive and fragile flowers of imagination—Gilberte and Albertine; in the other radiating from a more ethereal centre—the romance of history and the stability of tradition merging into maternal protectiveness—and finally dispersing into the void when Oriane de Guermantes is seen as herself and not as the incarnation of an imagined Geneviève de Brabantes and all the mother-mistresses who inhabit the faery landscapes of romantic prose.

Beauty loved and betrayed first through desire and then through social ambition; beauty finally abstracted from the experiences of these and fixed in the enchantment of style; this is the foundation pattern on which the book is built. 'And even in my most carnal desires, always pointing in a certain direction, concentrated about a dream essentially the same, I might have recognized as the first cause an idea, an idea to which I would have sacrificed my life, and at the most central point of which, as in my reveries during the afternoons when I used to read in the Combray garden, was the idea of perfection.'

The symmetry of the pattern is clearly to be seen in the early draft of the passage on the two 'ways' published by *La Table ronde* in 1945.

'On the Méséglise way I learned that to awaken love in our heart it is enough for a woman to have looked long at us and made us feel she might be ours; but on the Guermantes way I learned that sometimes to awaken our love it is enough for a woman to have looked away from us and made us feel she never could be ours.' These two women were to become Gilberte and Oriane. The situation was to be changed—Marcel was to misinterpret Gilberte's gesture of amorous invitation for one of contempt, and the look of kindness and promise was to be given to Mme de Guermantes. But the principle of crystallizing the imaginative experience of early life round two centres, represented by the two 'ways', was to be maintained and to provide the main articulation of the novel's skeleton.

This same draft goes on to describe an experience of involuntary memory. On the way to Combray one year, the narrator hears the clink of hammer on steel as the gangers work on the railway lines. It is a moment of spiritual depression when he has lost all sense of beauty or desire. Later in his holiday, picnicking with his governess in the woods, the sound of a fork striking a plate recalls the earlier moment; again he sees the landscape from the train window, but differently. Seen by the intelligence or remembered by the intelligence the view had been 'insipid'; re-created through sensation, nature seemed 'alive, lived, past, intoxicating and lovely'. And Proust offers his explanation; the sense of beauty is dependent on the apprehension of an 'extra-temporal truth' arising from the exact correspondence of a present moment with a past moment.

This incident and the explanation offered by Proust subsist in the later novel, but they are postponed to Marcel's middle age. This postponement is the first and most important of the steps by which the embryo plan grew into the final design, and it is worth tracing the other steps as far as we can. Not in the order in which they were made; the evidence is lacking, and it is more revealing to follow rather their logical order.

In the later plan the revelation of a kind of eternity through involuntary memory is postponed, multiplied into a series of instances, and shown as the culmination of a more sustained

33

and more dramatically effective rhythm; for the moment of spiritual impercipience is no longer an isolated moment, a mood, but the nadir of a slow spiritual decline. The reader has been prepared long since for the idea of this spiritual wasting, for it figures largely in the explanation of Swann's artistic infertility in the first two volumes, and it was perhaps with the introduction of this scheme of decline, death and resurrection that Proust came to see how certain religious notions could be adapted to his purpose and how some ready-made patterns of emotional response which, in so many contemporary minds, were inhibited by the intellectual refusal of religious experience could be released in the more acceptable context of the religion of art. 'Resurrection', he wrote in *Sodome et Gomorrhe*, 'is perhaps a phenomenon of memory.' Not only did he splendidly recapture the sublime of the perennial notion that an artist lives on in his work, the notion which had obsessed Mallarmé and which Proust expresses in the passage on the death of Bergotte; he imported reincarnation, successive deaths and final resurrection in the eternal into the scheme of life itself as lived by a creative artist, by emphasizing the discontinuity between the different epochs of Marcel's affective life—Marcel before and after his grandmother's death, Marcel in and out of love with successive women—while showing the spiritual continuity which underlies the epochs and finally abstracting and systematizing their spirituality in the 'resurrection' of *Le Temps retrouvé*.

The moment before the revelation, when Marcel hears the ganger's hammer ringing on the metal of the carriage wheel and thinks dispiritedly of the beauty he ought to be seeing in the dappled trees, is the end of his spiritual decline; the peak from which life falls away is Combray and childhood, the time of greatest spiritual vitality, imaginative spontaneity and confidence in life. Between these two terms come the repeated attempts to convert into the acts of living, into immediately real and solid substance, the spiritual experiences glimpsed through literature or in the solitary enjoyment of natural beauty. Each attempt is frustrated; after each Marcel is thrown back upon his solitude and the increasing conviction that spiritual value is nowhere to be found outside himself except where his own imagination has projected it. But imagination itself loses its conviction and its power; Marcel is less and less convinced that there is any transcendence to be hankered after, and less and less able to bring about the illusion whereby it may be pursued in a woman or a landscape; in the last stage of imaginative debility he cannot even find it in art itself. As imagination fades faith and the intuition of purpose fail with it. This withering ends in what is virtually a spiritual death; and in the first of the two volumes of *Le Temps retrouvé* the theme of decay and disintegration, of a world grown dreary and passionless, is sustained and amplified until, at the end of the volume, the curve begins to mount rapidly towards the counter-theme of revelation and resurrection, while

34

the sense of transformation and renewal is heightened by the continuing, in counterpoint, of the theme of decadence pursued now in connection, not with Marcel's spiritual life, but with the effects on other people of the time from which Marcel is on the point of escaping into his own kind of eternity.

This brings us to the (logically) next step in the elaboration of the novel's plan; for the revelation, though it is dramatically important for it to present itself in a rapid series of lightning-flashes, must be prepared if it is to win the reader's assent. It must be prepared, and the preparation must be, as far as possible, clandestine. Illumination must be retrospective; the light of the flashes must irradiate the country over which the reader has travelled; mysteries must be made plain, but they must first of all be mysteries. And so firstly, Marcel's spiritual decline is accompanied by a frustrated and declining sense of literary vocation. Secondly, this downward curve is offset by another —the curve of Marcel's understanding and appreciation of literature, painting and music through contact with the works and personalities of artists, which rises steadily until the approach to the moment of crisis. Then it reverses its direction, to move steeply downwards with the other curve towards the stay with Gilberte de Saint-Loup at Tansonville, when the two 'ways' with their individual auras of magic are shown to have become one stretch of dreary countryside, and a passage supposed to have been found among unpublished portions of the Goncourt diary finally shakes Marcel's belief in his own vocation and faith in art itself. Thirdly, the essential characteristics of the predestined artist in Marcel are thrown into relief, when they are at last revealed, because Proust has drawn in a number of near-artists and shown (though this is apt to be unnoticed except in retrospect or perhaps more often, in practice, on a second reading) the elements which these incomplete artists lack and which Marcel is eventually shown to possess. The most important instance of this is Swann. Marcel is able to grasp firmly and finally a spiritual reality which had dangled just outside Swann's reach.

This design gave Proust complete liberty to introduce into his book every feeling and every idea derived from the dialogue between his own spiritual self-exploration and the various forms of the romantic-symbolist mysticism of art. Under the guise of showing love as an illusion, a debased ideal, he could exercise to the full his capacity for the lucid, detailed and most unmystical observation and notation of the movements of his own emotions; the meticulous detail could be fitted (though not without a certain amount of intellectual evasion) into the grand pattern, richly related to traditional religious patterns, of spiritual destiny conceived in terms of the gulf between the eternal and the temporal and culminating in the redemption of the temporal through art. Time becomes the key to destiny, becomes fate itself; everything connected with the effects of time and change becomes relevant to the general scheme; man is great because he bears the weight of time and twice great when, as artist, he can create his own means of salvation.

Just as the idea of love as illusion allows Proust to extend his clinical study of its emotions and link the tradition of Constant and Stendhal to that of Chateaubriand, Baudelaire and the Symbolists, the idea of social ambition as the pursuit of poetry allows him to satisfy his ambition, based on his admiration for La Bruyère, Saint-Simon and Balzac, to survey the society of his day—or that region of society which was all he himself could pretend to know. And here, moreover (and in spite of Proust's careful distinction, in *Le Temps retrouvé*, between the truth of art and the truth of science), Proust unites in himself the two great intellectual trends of the nineteenth century, Idealism and Positivism; for he is at once an Idealist expressing his own Idealism and a Positivist dissecting and explaining his own Idealism, though always, if not always consistently, explaining it in terms which leave the way open for a spiritual rather than a materialistic interpretation of ultimate reality. A. N. Whitehead observed that since the Renaissance the idea of scientific determinism has taken the place of the Greek fate. Nineteenth-century writers had various ways of dealing with the increasing sense of imprisonment in mechanical process. Mallarmé admitted that there was no place for the spirit in the natural cosmos and affirmed that humanity had created spirit and could learn to make its own world of it. Proust portrays a similar dichotomy in terms of the hostility between subjective spirituality and reality outside the self; a reality which, he appears to believe, we can never know in itself, but which, whenever illusion fails, we must always realize to be at best indifferent and at worst hostile to the subject. The process of human destiny, seen from the outside, is repetitive and meaningless. But Proust, like so many of his contemporaries—like Hardy, for instance—is fascinated by the circling juggernaut of time; and just as in Greek tragedy the greatness of man is measured by the greatness of the forces which oppress him, in the final volumes of *A la recherche* we hear more and more of the 'great laws' which govern those patterns of human vicissitudes from which art is the refuge. There are laws which apply to individual experience—the laws of love, the laws which govern all the relationships between imagination and reality. But laws apply also to the evolution of groups; groups decline and are renewed, and with renewal comes change. The *grand monde* declines and is renewed through an infiltration of the *bourgeoisie* which changes its character—superficially at least, and perhaps only superficially. None of these changes is progressive; within groups the lives of individuals follow the same basic patterns; behind every individual is massed a great thrust of determinism. Heredity, for instance, loomed almost as large in Proust's mind as it did in Zola's, different as his treatment of it is. Swann, as he grows older, falls into the habits and ways of thought of his Jewish ancestry; Marcel feels his father's character growing again within himself.

The difficulty was to assimilate these 'laws' into the philosophical explanation of art which was to follow the revelation and crown the work. For this explanation was to be in essence anti-intellectual, or at least (since the intellect is allowed a large part in the act of writing) anti-conceptual; and the laws in which Proust was so interested are, however arrived at, conceptual. The reconciliation was difficult and no doubt accounts for much of the confusion of ideas in *Le Temps retrouvé;* in so far as it can be said to have been effected at all, the trick depends on the ambiguity of the word 'idea'. One sense is that of the Symbolists, where the idea is the abstraction from lived experience of certain affective components which can be held in the mind apart (to some extent at least) from the particular occasions which gave rise to them. In this sense lyrical art can be held to be the expression of 'ideas', of the aesthetic essence of experiences, and the notion can be given a Platonic or Hegelian or Bergsonian twist. The other sense is that of the idea as an intellectual pattern in which relationships are logical and in no degree affective. Here, to arrive at the idea of a process is to understand its nature; and Proust justifies the need to arrive at such ideas within his scheme of salvation by proposing the notion that to understand the nature of one's suffering is to escape from it. Schopenhauer wrote of the 'ideas' of art as an escape from flux, but he used the word in the first rather than the second sense. Spinoza had said that an emotion ceases to be an emotion as soon as we form a clear and distinct idea of it. Proust proposes two kinds of enjoyment: the perpetuation of transcendent pleasure through involuntary memory and the escape from remembered suffering through understanding. Both are, in a sense, abstractions from experience; but the one is the abstraction of feeling, the other of principles. Both abstractions are functions of the intellect; but in the first case the intellect must be prevented from abstracting its own aesthetically irrelevant patterns and omitting the concrete and intellectually irrelevant detail of the impression.

So far we have seen the plan in the abstract, built on the foundation of Combray and the two 'ways'. In the imagination of Marcel as a child, Swann's way stands for a world beyond the familiar world of family life. Outside, unknown, existing as a steadily growing set of imaginative assumptions is a world of artistic culture, which is closed to Marcel's family, and of romantic sexual love frowned on by the *vertus de Combray*. The imagination of a world of artists and artistically cultured people is centred in the unknown figure of Bergotte; the imagination of sexual adventure in the unknown figure of Swann's daughter, Gilberte. Swann is, at first, the only contact with both except for Bergotte's books; and both are interrelated by the thought of Gilberte's friendship with Bergotte. In the imaginative halo which surrounds the unknown Gilberte are reflected the colours which glow in Bergotte's prose; later, when Marcel has met and fallen in love with the real Gilberte, Bergotte's halo reflects the colours of Marcel's romantic passion. Marcel, through his acquaintance with Gilberte, explores the reality of the Swann *milieu*, and begins to explore the experience of love on the mental and physical planes; the world of literary culture, Bergotte and all, is, as a way of life, disappointing, and so is love.

Similarly, the Guermantes way is associated with the poetry of history, lineage, aristocracy and a more rarefied, more maternally protective, less sensual love. Marcel again makes his way into the corresponding reality and is disillusioned.

The two ways are made the assembly-points, as it were, for the features of Marcel's imaginative life, and organized into two sets of ambitions, each of which is to be realized. They are distinct, and stand for two socially distinct worlds into which Marcel successively penetrates. At the end of the Combray episode they divide, and we move first into Swann's world, then into the Guermantes'; but they are connected in their division by a complicated web of individual relationships which multiply and pull them together again in *Le Temps retrouvé*. When Marcel goes to visit Gilberte and her husband at Tansonville, he realizes how the two ways, so distinct in his childish imagination, connect on the map—sees, too, how empty they are of the poetry with which in childhood he had invested them; until at last these two kinds of poetry themselves draw together in the beatific vision of Combray re-created in art. Their distinct poetries meet in Marcel's subjectivity as their geographical realities connected in gloomy reality on the map. And the two social worlds for which they stand are united; Gilberte, whom, in Swann's lifetime, Oriane de Guermantes refused to receive, is married to Oriane's nephew; the Princesse de Guermantes is now Mme Verdurin, the apparently inverted snob of Swann's own social stratum; and the guests are a motley collection of aristocracy, bourgeoisie and nondescripts.

If the middle sections of the novel had not been so inflated during the years of the war when publication was suspended, the abstract symmetry of the plan would have been reflected in the physical symmetry of the divisions of the book; distributed over two or three volumes, we should have had *Du côté de chez Swann* and *Le côté de Guermantes* in roughly equal dimensions, preceded by Combray and rounded off with the account of Marcel's revelation, originally to be called *L'Adoration perpétuelle*.

The movement of Marcel's consciousness of experience is, generally speaking (to use the expression applied by Ramon Fernandez to the development of Marcel's notion of the Guermantes) that of a 'poetic nebula which slowly crystallizes and cools into ideas'. The aesthetic satisfaction Proust proposed to himself was to recover, as far as possible, the nebula and to illustrate the ideas. To concentrate the nebula, he arranged the memories of his own childhood and filled in the gaps in the pattern, wonderfully re-creating within himself the eye and soul of a child, but never losing the lucidity, critical power and irony of an adult intelligence; to demonstrate his laws, he stylized his psychology of the passions he knew best, arranging and creating according to the principles he set out to demonstrate; with a marvellous fidelity of detail, but omitting whatever of human love did not fit his pattern and, *a fortiori*, whatever of human love did not come within the purview of his own experience.

IV

Combray

In *Le Temps retrouvé*, Proust complains that the critics who read the first part of his book spoke of his microscopic scrutiny of his mind 'whereas I had, on the contrary, used a telescope to descry things which were indeed very small, but because of their great distance, and each of which was a world'. Marcel, looking backwards, sees a succession of different selves, and each of them inhabiting his own world, with its own particular atmosphere and key sensations; the word itself connects with the famous sentence of the introduction: 'A sleeping man has round him in a circle the succession of hours, the order of years and worlds'. The epoch when he first explored the Faubourg Saint-Germain was one of these worlds; Balbec was another; the Champs-Elysées and Gilberte's home were another. The most self-contained, the brightest, the sun from which all other worlds borrowed some degree of reflected light, was Combray. Whenever Marcel looks for the origin of those values, attitudes and expectations which set the course of his life and determine the measure of his happiness, it is to Combray that he must return; and when he comes to present his past in the radiance of involuntary memory, it is round Combray that the halo shines most convincingly.

Combray, with its two ways, was artificially constructed out of the significant features of Proust's childhood. Into it went memories of his life in Paris itself, at his uncle's house at Auteuil and at his Aunt Amyot's house at Illiers. Illiers played by far the largest part. P.-L. Larcher, in *Le Parfum de Combray*, shows just how much (and how little) the actual topography of Illiers contributed to Proust's reconstruction; the rest was invented by Proust to correspond with what he remembered of his imaginative life and with the pattern of this as he ordered and completed it in transforming his own past into Marcel's. According to Léon Pierre-Quint, Proust could never spend his summer holidays in the country after his first bad attack of asthma at the age of nine, and went instead to the coast. But memories of sea, coast and seaside resorts were reserved for the second 'world' of natural impressions, Balbec, which was to show the second of the two most creative phases in Marcel's spiritual history. Into the stylized topography and partly imagined family and inhabitants of Combray, Proust packed all his childhood memories, up to early adolescence, which in retrospect appeared to be connected with his moral failure and artistic success. The year is limited to late spring, summer and early autumn. Marcel's is a life of freedom from school and social contacts with people of his own age. The surroundings which reflect and stimulate his imagination are natural instead of urban. Leisure, independence and solitude limit the story of his growth to the story of the use he made of the freedom of his imagination.

People are part of the child's background. Proust had a brother, Robert; Marcel has none. He is dispensed from the frictions and adjustments which Proust had known. Elisabeth de Gramont wrote of the division of Proust's family into two clans: Marcel and his mother, sensitive and easily moved; Robert and his father, sane, stable, conventional and impatient of the hyperaesthesia of the others. In *Jean Santeuil* there is no brother, but there are distractingly normal cousins, from whom Jean Santeuil has to shut himself away in a manner which, to the unsympathetic reader, might appear frowsty and perhaps disagreeably unsociable; in *A la recherche*, the room with drawn blinds or the deep hooded chair in the garden are part of the idealized and dreamlike privacy of Marcel's natural solitude, accepted and savoured in isolation from the world of social obligations. Most of the people who live close to Marcel are two generations away in time: the grandmother and her two sisters, Céline and Flora, the grandfather, his brother Adolphe (soon cut off from the family by his supposed indiscretion in introducing Marcel to his flighty mistress, Swann's future wife Odette de Crécy) and his cousin, Marcel's great-aunt, who owns the Combray house. The others are a generation away: his parents and Aunt Léonie, great-aunt's daughter, who becomes a permanent invalid from the time when her husband, Uncle Octave, dies.

If, to the child, these people are part of his background, the moral forces with which he has to reckon and from which he draws his first impressions of the world of adult responsibilities and relationships, to Proust they are puppets in the human comedy. They share with the dreamlike quality of a world supposedly recovered by involuntary memory the shadowy yet over-rigid, inconsequential yet over-typical character of their words and habits; they are not quite in tune—the grandmother particularly—with the moral exigencies and ideals which for the child they represent. For they and the whole of the Combray episode are seen with the double vision which, in one form or another, is characteristic of Proust. One form of the double vision here is that the child's divinities are felt by the child as divinities and seen and appraised by the grown man as equals (or, subtly, as inferiors); another is that Proust, always capable of seeing his own character sympathetically from the inside and critically from the outside, condemning his vices while he was frustrated as a writer but more inclined to rationalize them when successfully writing because he saw the interconnection between his weakness and his genius, tended to reserve for Marcel all of himself that could be idealized and connected with genius and to project into other characters, sometimes recommended for tolerance and sympathy but sometimes mocked, gently or cruelly, the comic or more obviously morbid or vicious sides of himself. And so illness and solitude, in so far as they mean sensitiveness, contemplation and reflection, are given to Marcel; in so far as they stand for hypochondria, self-indulgence and the shelving of responsibility they are indulgently caricatured in Aunt Léonie, 'perpetually lying in a vague state of sorrow, physical weakness, illness, obsession and devotion', Aunt Léonie to whom Marcel, in *La Prisonnière*, finds himself growing closer in temperament and habits as his illness increases its hold upon his life.

If, for Proust, these adult characters are the butts of his indulgent humour, the childish perspective of them which he attributes to the young Marcel is dominated by three impressions: the love and solicitude of his grandmother and his mother, their moral rectitude and even, in his grandmother, idealism, together with the guilty sense of how far he falls short of the standards they propose, and the gratuitous cruelty which these grown-ups sometimes show each other. Céline and Flora bate their sister by offering her husband forbidden brandy and calling her to see him drink; Françoise is as brutal to the pregnant kitchen-maid as she is to the chickens she enjoys killing. Happiness and security depend on the affection of his mother and grandmother; and the symbol of this too close dependence on maternal protectiveness is the good night kiss of which he is deprived on the evenings when Swann comes to dine. There comes an evening, no doubt real enough in Proust's life, for it begins *Jean Santeuil* and figures again in the draft published by *La Table ronde*, when the child must at all costs have his good night kiss. Since the greatest suffering of an otherwise secure and happy life is the nightly separation from his mother, the ideal is to force the issue and demand the viaticum. Which he does, only to discover that he has ruined for himself another ideal by failing to control one of those nervous impulses which those who most care for him see as the most pressing danger to his moral life and future happiness. The child takes what solace he can from the notion that his defection comes more from his nerves than himself, but cannot rid himself of the guilt of disappointing his mother. Calm, escape from guilt and quiet enjoyment of his mother's presence come only when George Sand's *François le Champi* has put a veil of lively if, to the child who only partly follows the story, obscure patterns of imagination between reality and himself. This is Marcel's first contact with romantic literature; the incident of the good night kiss is the first instance of the escape from reality into imagination which is the direction of art, the direction of life being, in general, the fall from imagination into the desert of reality. The anguish of the child, morover, is connected, by Proust, with the anguish which for Swann, and an older Marcel, is an essential part of the experience of love.

Proust, since he paids so much attention to this incident, seems to have remembered it more readily and vividly than any other part of his childhood. It is a perfect introduction to the temperamental qualities of the narrator, and it is magnificently dramatic writing. What might, in cold blood, appear a molehill makes a most convincing mountain; and the moral dilemma it symbolizes must indeed have been crucial for Proust himself. Over-sensitive and suffering children have lately infested literature, but impatience can hardly project itself back on to Proust. Whatever may now seem banal in the situation is redeemed by many things: the obvious artistic sincerity which marks successful communication of feeling without sentimental comment; the distance which the narrator puts between the experience and his present self, the cool detachment with which, paradoxically, the drama is conveyed—another aspect of that duality which is characteristic of Proust's attitude to his material; the emotional subtlety of the presentation, assuming guilt, yet forcing sympathy and the reader's connivance—Baudelaire's 'hypocrite lecteur' less brutally and more insidiously proposed; above all, perhaps, the sense of revelation of intimate mysteries which has been built up by the introduction. This crux of Proust's moral failure, this epitome of the moral drama diluted in the narratives of *Les Plaisirs et les jours*, is bathed now in a serenity reflected from Proust's sense of his achievement of *l'adoration perpétuelle*. He has won his battle on ground of his own choosing.

In *Le Temps retrouvé*, Proust wrote that the deeper the artist has to plunge within himself to recover the impressions to be recorded, the denser will be the poetic atmosphere with which they are surrounded. It is in his introduction, leading into the world of Combray, that Proust makes artistic use of the mystery, effort and final sense of reward which attend the recovery of past impressions. At the outset, we wait outside the Ali Baba's cave of the unconscious. Humblot, the manager of the publishing house of Ollendorff, waited impatiently, unable to understand, he reported, why a man need take thirty pages to describe his tossings and turnings on the verge of sleep. The more patient reader, catching the rumour of intriguing doings within, is given glimpses of the range of partial consciousness from civilization to brutishness and back, mentions of the riches which, later, he is to possess—Combray, Balbec, Paris, Doncières, Venice—then a full view of one moment of the Combray ritual.

the incident of the good night kiss. After the mounting tension and release of the child's anguish, the assault on the door of Marcel's past begins again; Marcel, at some undefined moment in middle life, tastes the *madeleine* soaked in tea, and slowly the door moves, to open wide at last on the vision of Combray seen from the approaching train, with the church in the foreground.

The atmosphere of apocalypse generated by the superb narrative of the *madeleine* incident and the introduction surrounds the whole of the Combray episode. The imperfect tense lifts even specific and apparently singular happenings out of the world of temporal succession; events and scraps of conversation are reported in this tense of habit and extension, of actions and feelings which are never thought of as ending in a recordable achievement; which, as parts of life, are irremediably lost, but, recovered in words, are the significant extensions and dimensions of the past's substance. 'I confess', wrote Proust, 'that a certain use of the imperfect—that cruel tense which shows us life as at once ephemeral and passive, which, at the very moment when it retraces our actions, marks them as illusions, annihilates them in the past without leaving us, as the perfect tense does, the consolation of activity—is always, for me, a source of mysterious moods of sadness.' Many events are thrust back into the pluperfect; seen, that is, not as part of the succession of a moving life but as subsisting only in their effects, in their lasting contribution to the tensions and assumptions which are part of Marcel's background.

The anguish of bedtime is the first sign of the serpent in Marcel's Eden, the first instance of the way in which events refuse to adapt themselves to wishes. There are other foreshadowings of a future to be lived in a fallen world. Yet Combray is stability and security, with its limitations offset by the freedom of a vivid and lively imagination nourished on books, and not yet aware that its failure to be self-sufficient promises disillusion. At this stage we are given the delight in the illusions themselves, the promises later to be betrayed.

Stability, security, tradition, habit, all these are summed up in the church solidly and comfortably ensconced in time, a visible and permanent past. The church is the first part of Combray to be seen, after Marcel's bedroom, and if we leave it to meet Aunt Léonie drinking her lime-flower tea we soon return to explore its detail. For it is a symbol of what the novel sets out to be; in *Le Temps retrouvé*, at the very end of the book, it reappears: 'This dimension of Time, of which I had had a presentiment in Combray church, I would try to make continually perceptible in a transcription of the world which would have to be very different from that provided by our misleading senses.' For Proust the only essence is that of destiny completed, the only contemplation of essence is the contemplation of the essence of a completed past. In *Le Temps retrouvé* his white-haired and wrinkled characters have achieved a kind of grandeur by achieving a past, their only real dimension. Combray church and Balbec church, symbols of Amiens and all the mediaeval churches to the significance of whose iconography Proust had been awakened by Ruskin and Mâle, are, like Proust's novel, means of renewing in contemplation a lost spiritual vigour.

The past is solidity; it is also romance. Every symbol of the past is a window for the imagination on to the glamour of legend. The ancient porch of the church gives access not only to the finger-worn holy water stoup, the tomb covering the noble dust of the abbots of Combray and the peacock colours of the windows, but, by suggestion, to a grotto hung with stalactites, a valley visited by fairies and the mystery of a Merovingian darkness. Stimulating to the imagination, yet static, familiar and unthreatening; offering the rich essence of time with none of time's menace of change, the church has the degree of its past extension marked in the varieties of its architecture and ornament, reflecting the preoccupations, tastes and spiritual qualities of many periods. And its steeple is the symbol of a world clear of Proust's oppressive sense of guilt, the centre of the *vertus de Combray*; they, the steeple and Marcel's grandmother are grouped together in Marcel's memory.

It is the privilege of childhood to combine routine and freedom, security and imaginative adventure; Marcel is so morbidly dependent on the familiar that he is a little afraid even of the freedom and adventure of imagination. The magic lantern which covers the walls of the bedroom where he suffers the prospect of the nightly separation from his mother with coloured pictures of Geneviève de Brabant's castle and Golo on horseback 'filled with dreadful purpose' is an intimation of supernatural mystery and beauty, but also an uncomfortable intrusion into the world of comfortable habit. There are, in the last event, only two ways in which Marcel can adjust imagination and reality; by dulling imagination through habit, or by escaping from reality into books. Habit is the drug which deadens the pain experienced by the imaginative self in a hostile reality.

But imagination is not to be denied; and between habit and art there lie the alternately ecstatic and dispiriting rhythms of illusion and disillusion. In the Combray episode, almost the whole of the child's world is caught up on the tide of poetry, as the doorknob and all the natural irregularities in the walls of Marcel's room are caught up out of their material function by the light of the magic lantern and absorbed into the 'supernatural essence' of Golo and his horse; this complex of the sensuous pleasure of colour, historical exoticism and the emotions connected with Golo's vaguely ominous descent on Geneviève's castle is one of the determinants of Marcel's imaginative life; it connects directly and in all its elements with the suggestiveness of the stained glass windows in the church, and the double complex is the source of the poetry which marks the beginning of what Marcel, using one of Bergson's terms, calls the '*durée*'

44

of the name Guermantes in his own mind—for Oriane de Guermantes is a descendant of the historical Geneviève. Elements drawn from his later imagining as stimulated by books gravitate towards and crystallize round this double nucleus; and before this particular poetic world is thrown off its orbit by the first sight of Oriane in the flesh, he is already more than half in love with her as he has created her for himself.

In the draft of *La Table ronde*, where the river Vivette, later to be the Vivonne, has already changed in character from the more realistic Loir of *Jean Santeuil*, Proust confesses that what he looked for in the Guermantes way was the magic countryside suggested by books like *Le Lys dans la vallée*. He looked, he said, in vain. Nature could not live up to the combined creativeness of Balzac's novel and Marcel's imagination. In *A la recherche*, the Guermantes way is made to the measure of the spiritual reality. In the draft, Proust wrote: 'In the characteristic colour assumed in memory by each separate year of my life, I cannot distinguish whether it was desire for the landscape which made me link a woman with it or whether it was love for the woman which made me desire the landscape.' In *A la recherche*, he refers often to that fusion of erethism with the sense of natural beauty which makes him long to possess the countryside physically in the person of a peasant girl who sums up her background in herself; but in the case of the imagined Oriane, where the notion of love is most rarefied, the poetry of the woman and of the 'way' with which she is associated has its earliest sources in colour, legend and books. Marcel's spiritual progress is from the Eden of reading to the fallen world of living and back to the paradise of a literature created, this time, by himself. It seems, moreover, that if the real Oriane de Guermantes was based on people like the Comtesse de Chevigné and Mme Strauss, the Oriane of Marcel's imagination may have been a relative of Balzac's Mme de Mortsauf, perhaps also of Stendhal's Mme de Rênal; and that the faery beauty of the Guermantes way was created by Proust's imagination dwelling in memories not only of Illiers but of the landscapes he read of in books—the river landscapes of *Le Lys*, of *Le Rouge et le noir*, of *Mademoiselle de Maupin*. Proust's notebooks, as they have so far been reported on, do not provide, like Coleridge's, the clues needed to investigate such imaginative transmutations in detail; but comparison of all these landscapes shows suggestive correspondences which it would take too long to detail here, and leads to the conclusion that Proust finally created in his own words the magic which other men's words had suggested to him and which, even to his childish and willing eyes, the real landscapes had appeared to lack.

And this suggests a reason for the main differences between the landscapes of *A la recherche* and *Jean Santeuil*. Jean's Etreuils, like Marcel's Combray, is based on memories of Illiers—indeed sometimes Proust forgets himself and writes 'Illiers' instead of 'Etreuilles'. Etreuilles is, in fact, nearer the reality. Compared with Combray, Etreuilles is one-sided. The prosy river Loir is the forerunner of the Vivonne, but there is only one 'way'. There is a Méséglise; there are long descriptions of hawthorn and apple-blossom; these flowers are already surrounded with significant emotional associations which Proust is exploring. But the hawthorns are not balanced by the water-lilies, and there is no question of the symbolic geography of the two ways. Of all the choice of explanations offered in *Le Temps retrouvé* for the transcendence of experience relived in memory, the most likely seems to be the freedom which memory leaves to the imagination to transpose the past as it will.

In *A la recherche*, too, the feeling of yearning after the past is kept within narrow bounds. It breaks through sometimes in a shaft of emotion which has gained in poignancy from its containment, as when Marcel suddenly leaps forward in time from the description of the Combray church to a moment when, in Paris, the sight of a spire recalls it, and he forgets the purpose for which he had asked a passer-by the way, to stand dreaming at the view and the memory: 'and no doubt then, and more anxiously than a moment ago when I asked for information, I am looking for the right way, turning down a street . . . but . . that street is in my heart'; or when, at the end of the account of Combray, he speaks of its beauties as the foundation of his aesthetic life: 'When on summer evenings the resounding sky growls like a wild beast and everyone is depressed by the storm, it is to the Méséglise way that I owe the ecstasy I alone know of breathing, through the sound of falling rain, the perfume of invisible and everlasting lilacs.'

The poignancy here is felt by a reader who has just seen and smelled the lilacs and known their beauty in the terms Marcel proposes. The vision which in *Jean Santeuil* is merely hinted at is here created. In *Jean Santeuil* the sea which, remembered, in beatitude, is, as described, a less-than-ordinary sea. The reference to it is brief; the novelist is concerned with the disembodied emotion of the experience, ineffable and only to be hinted at in terms which are little more than the abstract signs of feeling. Etreuilles is described in detail, and the poetry of the hawthorn and lilacs of Combray is there in germ. But it is a daylight and unframed picture of Jean's early summers. The 'worlds' of *A la recherche* which are to corrrespond most closely with the evocations of unconscious memory, and which are also to be shown as the occasions and crystallizers of the narrator's awareness of his own poetry—Combray and Balbec—are created in sensuous terms and bathed in a dreamlike atmosphere which carries over something of the mystery of the introduction.

And with the satisfaction of creating an ideal world, the yearning passes into the background of Proust's mind. His imagination is no longer dispersing itself painfully into the void, but exercising itself to make good the gaps in the writer's present world. Not merely remembering, with whatever kind of memory, a past as it *really* was, in whatever sense of 'really', but shaping an ideal present in terms of the best of the past. At last Proust is not crying for the moon, but making his own, in his own—the artist's—way.

A la recherche, then, adds to the earlier Etreuilles the Guermantes way with its complex of associations—the magic lantern, the church windows, books—all concentrated into a magnetic attraction towards Oriane. It also develops and organizes the complex of associations centred on the Méséglise—later called Swann's—way. Books again—Bergotte's here, with ironic but significant overtones of *Phèdre*—the hawthorns of Tansonville; the magnetism of the image of Gilberte. The central image here is the hawthorns, which draw their power from an associative complex of their own. In *Jean Santeuil* their associations are lucidly probed and baldly stated; in *A la recherche* merely suggested. But the early version confirms the importance of the suggestions and the deliberation with which they were worked into the pattern.

The hawthorns are white and pink; the order of impact in the main passage to which we must refer is white hawthorn, pink hawthorn, Gilberte. Pink had a particular and particularly important emotive power for Proust; *Jean Santeuil* shows how clearly he realized it and how curious he himself was to know why. In this early book pink is first singled out for attention in connection with the magic lantern. In *A la recherche* the magic lantern, appropriated to the Guermantes complex, has another colouring; Geneviève wears a blue sash, Golo is dressed in red; but the striking colour is yellow—the yellow of the *landes* and of Geneviève's castle—and yellow the name Guermantes will always be for Marcel. Yellow, it naturally is, he further claims, playing in symbolist fashion with the notion of fixed correspondences between sensations of different orders and their significances; but the private mental association is established by the magic lantern. In *Jean Santeuil*, the pink of the magic lantern is connected with the pink biscuits served after lunch at Etreuilles; it is the colour associated with things which the child thinks delicious and exciting to eat; it is eminently sensual.

It returns, in *Jean Santeuil*, in the pink hawthorn. For Jean, as far back as he can remember, pink hawthorn is the epitome of spring, and its beauty the symbol of spring's sensations and the focus of his earliest desire. He proposes a choice of explanations without himself choosing. Were they really more beautiful than others, these flowers, so delicate in structure and vivid in colour that they seemed made for festive occasions—were indeed massed on the altar for the festive Month of Mary? Was it the intellectual pleasure of comparing them with the white variety, the double with the single, and noting at once the analogies and the distinctions? Hardly this, since he had seen dog-roses before seeing roses proper and had felt no comparable delight in that case. Was it because the white and pink hawthorn reminded him of cream cheese plain and cream cheese flavoured and coloured with crushed strawberries? Was it because, when he was ill in bed, his mother had brought him branches of pink hawthorn which had to stand for the spring landscapes he could not go out to see?

This method of probing is familiar even in *A la recherche*, where it subsists chiefly in the analysis of psychological motive, all possible explanations being mooted but none finally and exclusively chosen. The associations of the hawthorn, however,—and of all the intensely imagined passages on Combray—are dealt with differently. The private associations are brought in, but they are made to bring with them a universal, perennial and sublimated spring. We are given, not the wherefores of the experience, but the experience itself, detached from the passing moments of its real possession and transformed into a climate and a place—into what Mallarmé would have called a *région où vivre*, a dwelling place of the mind.

To trace the springs of the flood of feeling released by the main description of the hawthorns and transferred by Marcel to Gilberte we have to go back to the long passage on the pleasures of reading. We shall have to consider this in greater detail in the next chapter, when we come to consider Marcel's vocation. Here we need only note that Proust builds up the impression of an imagination which, stimulated by books, is confidently forward-looking and hopeful, turned towards a future vague, but compact of pleasures known, pleasures unknown and anticipated, and pleasure and knowledge beyond what is already known or specifically imagined. 'My dreams of travel and love were only moments—which today I isolate artificially as if I were cutting sections at different heights in a fountain of water, rainbow-coloured and seemingly motionless—in an identical and inflexible upspringing of all the force of life within me.'

Almost immediately afterwards these pleasures of reading are attached to the name of Bergotte. What is particularly emphasized here is the notion of transcendence. In Bergotte, for the first time, transcendence is associated with style; for Marcel, as we shall see, has later to realize that transcendence can *only* be achieved in style. But, for the purpose we are now considering, Bergotte's name is firmly established as a password to the heaven of Marcel's imagining.

Bergotte has written on *Phèdre*. This is first mentioned quite casually, as one of the books and natural features of which Bergotte's style had 'revealed' the beauty to Marcel; but gradually, when Bergotte's name is mentioned, his pamphlet on Racine is brought into the foreground. One importance of this is in connection with the later development of the theme of Marcel's understanding of art; *Phèdre* is the chief role of La Berma, and after the pretentious nonsense talked about that actress by Norpois it is Bergotte who will reveal to Marcel the

48

beauty of La Berma's acting. But Phèdre also provides overtones to Marcel's passion, first for Gilberte, then for Albertine.

Next, Bergotte's name is linked with Gilberte's; they go off together, as Marcel learns from Swann, to visit historic towns, cathedrals and castles which, for Marcel, add their romantic associations to the names of the two people. It is then that Marcel begins to fall in love with the unknown girl.

Soon afterwards the hawthorn theme is introduced; here they are white, and first seen on the church altar in celebration of the Month of Mary. But the images worked into their detailed description bring in a series of associations ranging from the religious to the frankly sensual: the church, the holy mysteries, festivity and marriage, nature and the life-force; the grace, liveliness and coquetry of girls; then, specifically, and by a cunning transition, Vinteuil's daughter; Marcel tries to enter by empathy into the very sense of the movement of the stamens, and finds in this the toss of the head of a 'white, careless and sprightly girl *('fille')*'. The next sentence ostensibly changes the subject: 'M. Vinteuil had sat next to us with his daughter *('fille')*'. By the repeated word, Mlle Vinteuil is connected with the flowers, and after the short digression on Vinteuil's modesty and shyness, hawthorns and girl return. The flowers, as Marcel leaves the church, suddenly turn from sight to perfume, the bitter-sweet smell of almonds; Marcel's fancy locates this perfume in little spots on the flowers' surface which are whiter than the rest, associates it with the taste of almond paste and with Mlle Vinteuil's freckles, then with the imagined taste of Mlle Vinteuil's skin. From the holy mysteries we have run down a scale which ends in natural sensuality and the bite of instinct:

> For all the silence and stillness of the hawthorn, this intermittent ardour [of their perfume] was like the murmur of their intense life with which the altar buzzed like a hedgerow under the visitation of the living antennae of which the observer was reminded by certain stamens nearly red in colour which seemed to have kept the springtime virulence, the irritant power, of insects now metamorphosed into flowers.

Thus is established a scale of feeling on which Proust has learned to play at will, and the way is prepared for the main passage on the hawthorns and their association with Marcel's passion for Gilberte.

This passage is part of the section on the Méséglise way. From the beginning of the section, the impression is infused with sensuousness, with suggestions of the physically voluptuous; but this voluptuousness is idealized and caught up into the realm of poetry. Not, however, without a certain tension between the poetic and the physical, between the delight in the present sense of beauty and the pull of desire on the plane of instinct.

The first intimation of the essence of the Méséglise way is

49

the smell of its lilacs. The leaves of the lilacs are hearts, but they are *les petits coeurs verts et frais*—little, green and all that *frais* suggests of youth, coolness and innocence. The flowers are exotic, oriental; they are minarets showing above the Gothic gable of the lodge; they are houris. But beside them the nymphs of a western spring would seem common—for the overtones of sensuality are immediately damped and modified by the suggestion that these houris are not divinized flesh as much as the figures fixed in 'bright, pure colours' by Persian miniaturists. Yet, in Marcel, the impression ends in the desire to possess, to embrace the lilacs as if they were women.

The lilacs are nearly over; from them we pass to the hawthorns, by way of the less obviously but no less deeply erotic images of the flower-fringed pool, dominated by the 'lakeside sceptre' of the gladioli, its sleeping waters 'irritated' by insects which remind the observant reader consciously and the rapid reader unconsciously of the 'springtime virulence, the irritant power, of insects now metamorphosed into flowers' attributed earlier to the scent of the hawthorns in the church. When, immediately afterwards, the main hawthorn passage begins, Proust picks up all the associations established before—the church, holy mysteries, festivity, nature, the grace and liveliness of girls. But here the idea of the transcendence of their beauty is clearly brought out. The white hawthorns, which Marcel sees first, are connected with the church; with decorated altars, stained glass windows, the traceries of the rood-loft and the window-frames. In the next paragraph comes the suggestion of a transcendent beauty of which these flowers are the obscure symbol, the intimation of a 'dimension outside life' the idea of which haunted Proust. And this ideal dimension is referred to in terms of music; the flowers are first perfume, then rhythm, then melody, with the inscrutable beauty of melody. Next, framed within Marcel's hands, they become a painting; and the lead into the passage on the pink hawthorns is a double comparison —that between the painter's sketch and the finished picture that between a piece of music played on the piano and the same work played by an orchestra. The two comparisons are the more closely linked by the use of the word 'colour' to distinguish the richness of the orchestra from the clear tone of the piano.

The increased richness of the pink hawthorns as compared with the white is conveyed in terms of more frankly sensuous imagery. The associations Proust found in his mind during the explorations of *Jean Santeuil* are here lightly suggested, and their matter-of-factness is offset by a deprecatory irony. The pink biscuits are mentioned, and the bathos is cushioned by an indulgently slighting reference to the aesthetic values of Combray. The mature Proust is again double-sighted; aware of the emotional importance of the pink colour, aware also of the bathetic nature of its associations and that to sophisticated colour sensibilities pink is a little crude and common. He man

ages, subtly, to admit the validity of the memories of pink biscuits and cream cheese with strawberries crushed in it, while
adopting a patronizing attitude to such naïve and materialistic
associations: and this attitude, at once admiring and conde-
scending, is extended to nature itself, 'nature which, spontaneous-
ly, had expressed [the festive intention] with the naïveté of a
village shopkeeper working at a wayside altar, overloading the
bush with these rosettes of too lush a pink, this provincial
"pompadour".' And, from the idea of something exciting to
eat in the eyes of a child, we pass to the idea of girls dressed
for a ball. Just as, earlier, the transition was from the perfume
of the hawthorns to the taste of Mlle Vinteuil's cheeks, here the
transition is from the flowers as girls dressed in pink to Gilberte,
with her reddish hair and her pink-freckled face. Just as at the
beginning of the passage on the Méséglise way Marcel longed
to embrace the lilacs, here he fixes on Gilberte a look in which
all his senses urge the capture of her, body and soul.

All these impressions which have been linked together are
now concentrated into the image of Gilberte; her name becomes
a magic talisman: everything that is mysterious in the impressions
themselves is now placed within the mystery of Gilberte's unknown personality; every kind of desire, from the immediately
sensual to the aspiration after the obscurely transcendent, is
concentrated into the desire for Gilberte: and her name is left
floating on the air, ready to be picked up, literally in mid-air,
when the story of Marcel's acquaintance with Gilberte is resumed in the second volume, thus connecting the two parts of
the love story with one of those links unconsciously operative
before they are consciously perceived, in the use of which
Proust is a conscious master.

And the last stage in the development of the hawthorn theme
is a half-suggestive, half-ironic reference to *Phèdre*: Marcel, on
the eve of his departure for Paris, is found by his mother em-
bracing the hawthorns as he would have liked to embrace the
lilacs, trampling his new hat and tearing his new coat as Phèdre
tore off her *vains ornements*. The Phèdre suggestions move forward into the rest of the novel with the story of Marcel's passion
for Gilberte and Albertine; the theme is wound up in *Albertine
disparue* with an overt and detailed analogy between Phèdre
and Marcel in which Proust interprets Racine's psychology
in his own terms.

Thus both the 'ways' bring together impressions in which
delight in the senses is both an immediate pleasure and the
suggestion of a more mysterious pleasure to be attained, a
transcendent pleasure with which the only communication
is through the imagination. In both cases Marcel places this
transcendent pleasure in a person, and the attainment of the
pleasure in the future. In the case of the *côté de Guermantes*, the
contribution of the imagination is greater, that of the senses less
than in the case of the *côté de chez Swann*. To each of these poetic

aspirations corresponds a lower reality: Marcel's longing for the Guermantes magic is paralleled by Legrandin's snobbery; his romantic love for Gilberte is paralleled by his own more grossly sensual response to the beauty of the countryside, by the lesbianism of Mlle Vinteuil and her friend, by the forward look to the time when women will be the 'interchangeable instruments of a pleasure always the same'. Like Musset, Proust was inclined to look at sexual passion with the eye of a Chamfort as well as the eye of a Rousseau.

V

Swann

In *Un amour de Swann*, Swann steps out of Marcel's background into the foreground of the picture. The transition here is a kind of trick, a rapid glossing over of the inconvenient fact that involuntary memory can have played no part in Marcel's knowledge of Swann's past; Marcel casually mentions that, as he lay in bed—a reference, not to the *madeleine* incident which is supposed to have given rise to the vision of Combray, but to the very beginning of the novel—he used to think of what others had told him of Swann's past. Many critics have complained of this interruption of the narrative of Marcel's life, the dislocation of the chronology, the shift of attention from one person to another. The fact is, of course, that to Proust Swann and Marcel were intimately linked. They are related in much the same way as the novelist C. and Jean Santeuil are related, though with some relations reversed. Proust had snatched success out of the jaws of frustration: Marcel is the successful self, Swann the frustrated self. The things which distinguish Swann from Marcel are just those things which marked Proust's progress from sterility to productiveness. Between *Jean Santeuil* and *A la recherche*, Proust seems to have conceived the plan of telling his whole story as a biography of Swann in the third person: at that stage, the love affair of Jean Santeuil and Françoise was transferred to Swann. Whether Swann was to be successful or no we do not know; but eventually he was kept to serve as a foil to Marcel.

The temperamental affinities between Swann and Marcel are more than hinted at in the first volume; but if Swann, like Marcel, is based on Proust's knowledge of himself, he is also modelled, as we saw earlier, on other real people, chiefly Charles Haas.

Swann's gifts of sensibility are similar to Marcel's. He is open to sensuous beauty and keenly aware of sensual pleasure. Both work their way into the world of the Faubourg Saint-Germain without the advantages of birth and connection. Both suffer from a spiritual decline, a loss of aspiration, of devotion to an ideal beauty. Both are re-awakened from their spiritual torpor by the music of Vinteuil; but Swann is given only a partial and ineffectual reminder of the transcendent world, the dimension outside life; Marcel is given the full revelation which enables him to overcome the defects of character which make Swann a failure: hedonism, passivity, intellectual inertia, self-centredness. Marcel learns to transmute the 'impressions' provided by his sensibility into their 'spiritual equivalent'; Swann is a hedonist content with the passive enjoyment of whatever the chance of life provides. Marcel, by intellectual effort, understands his own suffering and the recurring pattern of his loves; Swann is obtuse and intellectually lazy, and *bears* his love affairs passively as outbreaks of an undiagnosed disease. Marcel willingly undertakes the painful effort of writing as an act of spiritual devotion and a sacrifice for the sake of mankind; Swann is mean in spirit and more than once behaves with a certain *muflerie*. Marcel sees the frivolity of high life and becomes an ascetic in order to write his book; Swann's ambition is reduced to that of introducing his daughter into the Guermantes circle. His attempts at creativity go no further than works like his little book on Vermeer, and he dies frustrated and unrealized. The parallel between Swann and Marcel is not blatant, but to the attentive reader it is pointed with precision.

From the moment when the conception of the novel took the form of the spiritual autobiography of a successful artist, Proust had left behind him a whole phase of his life, a phase marked by guilt and frustration: one can say perhaps that the leftovers of this phase are worked into the story of Swann, who, artistically speaking, misses salvation. He is given the destiny marked out for Proust by his friends and critics in the nineties —that of a dilettante. The phases of his love affair with Odette are almost exactly the phases of Marcel's; but he marries his mistress instead of art. *Un amour de Swann*, then, is tied in to the main structure; but it and the main structure could do without each other. It could have stood as a novel on its own: the rest of the book could have followed on without it. But as now arranged, the two are linked by innumerable cross-references connected with Swann, Odette and the Verdurins, and the foundations of the social history theme are laid in this part of the book; after which the emphasis shifts back to Marcel's spiritual autobiography.

In the Combray section Proust has set up the imaginative structures of the two passions which are to meet the check of reality. In Part III of *Du côté de chez Swann* he makes ready to introduce the theme of the disparity between imagination and reality explicitly, at first on a small scale. Having built up the complicated poetries of Oriane and Gilberte, he turns to the simpler images and associations of a number of place names, one of which is Balbec. These mental entities also are to meet the check of material reality. In the first plan of the book, the section called 'Place Names: the Name' was to be followed almost immediately by another called 'Place Names: the Place'. In the cutting and transposing made necessary by the inordinate size of the first projected volume, the original *Swann's Way*, and the redistribution and expansion which took place during the war, the second of the two titles disappeared. It is in *A l'ombre des jeunes filles* that the real Balbec comes to disturb Marcel's preconceptions.

Having set up the properties for this sequence near the end of the new *Swann's Way*, Proust returns immediately to the earlier sequence connected with his passion for Gilberte. And the continuity of this resumption with the earlier section is achieved with miraculous effect by a simple expedient, that of picking up Gilberte's name where, in the first part, it was left: floating in the air—of the Champs-Elysées, now, instead of the Tansonville garden. The correspondences between the two passages—of reflective comment, imagery, even phrasing—are striking; it is as though Proust were deliberately knotting the new thread on to the old—as, no doubt, he was.

Thus we begin the story of the reality of Marcel's love for Gilberte, which takes us over into *A l'ombre des jeunes filles*. The imagined Gilberte is detached from the real Gilberte and perishes, though ready for rebirth in a new shape and in connection with another girl. The imagined Bergotte is also detached from the real Bergotte. After the extinction of Marcel's love for Gilberte comes the journey to Balbec, and the imagined Balbec is detached from the real.

But these successive examples of the gulf between imagination and reality are not monotonous or uniform. If, in some cases, the reality is a dead weight of disillusion, in others there is a recovery. For instance, Marcel has romantic and sentimental notions of how charity, envy and justice should be represented in human form by a painter; when he sees Giotto's Virtues and Vices for the first time they seem to bear no relation to what they are supposed to represent—they are too solid, real and earthy to connect with his high-flown emotions. Later he comes to understand that their effectiveness as artistic expression lies in their very earthiness, their physical immediacy. Marcel goes to Balbec and is disappointed in its church and its sea until Elstir opens his eyes to their real beauty and significance. He goes to see La Berma play Phèdre, and is merely depressed by his own incapacity to be moved, until Bergotte has closed his mind both to his own irrelevant expectations and the would-be appreciative but equally irrelevant comments of Norpois.

In these cases, the sense of disillusion arises from a maladjustment which is to be blamed as much on a naïve imagination as on a defective reality, and to be corrected by the maturing of sensibility and understanding. Thus the older Marcel is able to trace the real connections between Bergotte the man and Bergotte the artist which, to his younger self, were at first invisible; and at the last he is able to see how art can achieve, in recorded contemplation, those states of mind which can finally satisfy the aspirations felt in childhood as a continuous up-springing of passionate expectation.

VI

The Artists

To convey his own notions about art and to show how these ideas were gradually and, at first, obscurely planted in Marcel's mind Proust invented four artists. In fact, he invented a great many; but those responsible for Marcel's education are Bergotte the novelist, Elstir the painter, Vinteuil the musician and La Berma the actress. In the case of these as of other characters in the novel we can look for, and find, originals; but in their case it is more interesting to look for the originals of their works. As characters, they fit into the pattern of Proustian society, but their human interest is slight. As people they have the transparency of their premeditated meaning; it is on their works that Proust lavishes his creative effort; their works be-come for the reader dense, familiar and real. Bergotte's we know only in fragments, since we never really get inside the covers of the one work of his which is mentioned by name, the pam-phlet on Racine; but Elstir's 'Port de Carquethuit' is almost as real to us as if we had seen it, and many of us are almost con-vinced we have heard Vinteuil's sonata and septet—perhaps that these are the loveliest things we have ever heard, which is at once ironic and tantalizing when we remember Proust's letter to Jacques de Lacretelle: 'The "little phrase" of the sonata is . . . the charming but infinitely mediocre phrase of a sonata for piano and violin by Saint-Saëns, a musician I don't like.' The passages on the 'little phrase' are based on the memory of a scrap of Saint-Saëns which *had once* moved Proust as the 'little phrase' in the novel moves Swann; but to this original impression Proust added others more recent and circumstantial —of fragments of *Parsifal* and *Lohengrin*, Franck's sonata and 'something of Schubert'. As finally presented, the account of Vinteuil's music is an attempt to concentrate Proust's sense of the very essence of music, felt in the mode of his time and interpreted according to the ideas of his time, ideas which he absorbed from sources as distinct as George Eliot and Schopenhauer.

Marcel's sense of vocation begins, naturally enough, with reading. In *Jean Santeuil*, reading is a pleasure which has to be defended against the pressures of a more active world; in *A la recherche* it is part of the accepted ritual of paradise. True, Mar-cel's grandmother attempts to dislodge Marcel from the shuttered bedroom into which the disembodied essence of summer filters with the rays of sunlight and the sound of Camus's hammering away at his packing-cases, as the disembodied

55

essence of travel reaches the narrator with the whistling of trains in the first pages of the novel, and the essence of the life of Balbec is to come to him behind the curtains of the Grand Hotel as he lies in bed, withdrawn, irresponsible and free to select and interpret sensation as his imagination wills; but grandmother's passion for fresh air has already been placed in the category of things to be laughed at and laughed away, and the vast hooded chair in the garden provides the essential amenities of inwardness combined with nearness to the concrete sensations of reality. This is Proust's ideal situation, the situation which his own style, 'poeticizing the real without transforming it', reflects.

But this 'poeticizing' itself is, in a sense, a transformation of the real; the real has to be filtered, concentrated and finally translated into language, into *cosa mentale*. Here, in these summer afternoons spent with books, withdrawal is a condition of the filtering and concentration of summer: 'The cool darkness of my room was to the full sunlight in the street as the shadow is to the sunbeam, just as luminous, that is, and offered my imagination the whole spectacle of summer which my senses, had I been out walking, could only have enjoyed in fragments.'

For Proust, eventually, withdrawal into the cork-lined room is to be the condition of the filtering and concentration of his life. On the selected and concentrated substance intellect and imagination are to work, expressing, but also embroidering and heightening. Here, at Combray, the embroidering and heightening are provided by the books Marcel reads. Against the background of the withdrawn mind, blank except for its sensuous well-being, situate nowhere but at the heart of summer, are to be enacted the events of mind-made worlds. These ideal realities, for Marcel, are the familiar ones, and from the consciousness of them he looks out almost as a stranger upon the concrete details of the summer scene from which his own mind has abstracted the essence. Between observed reality and his mind there is always an opaque film.

The first lesson, then, is that the writer's purpose is to create a kind of reality which, because it is mental in its nature, the mind can assimilate. The writer's first step, moreover, must be to detach his creation from life as it is lived. Real people are as opaque as real things; the real emotions of other people can only reach us through an intermediary—Proust writes 'through an image', but what he means includes, no doubt, all the means of the language of art, which he is later to discuss in terms of metaphor. These images, unlike the emotions of real people, can become as meaningful as the images of our own dreams; the emotions they awaken, like the emotions of dreams, are in fact amplified beyond anything we experience in life; they can be modulated at a speed beyond the resources of life, and therefore can show us truths about our own life whose truth we could not otherwise have felt—for instance, that our 'heart', our very way of feeling and desiring, changes, but too slowly, in life, for us to notice it. Here, in fact, Proust is modelling a general idea into a particular shape, coaxing it into a form which will be seen to correspond directly with one of the characteristics of his own book.

He goes on to say that if people, in the novels Marcel reads, are at once unlike the real people one knows but significant of the essence of humanity, the landscapes they live in are different in quality from any Marcel knows at Combray, and seem to be a part of nature itself. What Marcel does not realize, at this stage (for in these passages on art, more obviously than in the rest of the novel, we are in the presence of two Marcels: the younger, amassing observations but only dimly understanding them, and the older who has finally come to understand and is explaining the younger man's observations as he presents them), is that the human experience he reads about seems to him more significant than his own, the landscapes more essential than his familiar ones, not because the characters are people of a kind he does not know, the landscapes of a kind he has not seen, but because they are being presented by an artist who has made their significance perceptible. At this stage, in fact, Marcel is prepared to (and will later) make the same mistake as Emma Bovary: to believe that there are people it would be as thrilling to know as to read his favourite books, places as satisfyingly beautiful as descriptions. Later Marcel, like Flaubert himself, will maintain that these delights are never to be found except in the mind, never to be achieved objectively except in style, which is a record of mind and a means of communication with other minds. This analogy, already referred to, is perhaps worth pursuing here, for it illuminates not only the intentions of Flaubert and Proust but a whole region of romantic assumptions about the relationship between life and art.

Flaubert, like Proust, was intimately related to the chief character of his best book, *Mme Bovary*. 'Emma Bovary is myself.' Like Proust also, he approached this character in a spirit of detached and critical analysis. But the relationship is not quite the same in both cases. Emma Bovary is, in a sense, an incomplete artist like Swann. She is infinitely more crude in her tastes, ideas and feelings than Swann is, but she is a creature who experiences life through senses keenly alive and with a vivid imagination. She is Flaubert's 'lower self', the self which throve on the sensationalism and imaginative debauchery of romantic literature. 'I too', wrote Flaubert, 'have lived on my nerves . . . and like a convict I still bear the brand of it.' Flaubert shows how, at her convent, Emma's imagination was stimulated and nourished by romantic literature. She reads *Paul et Virginie* and imagines herself living their pure and innocent love, their idyllic passion combined with sentimental morality and modesty amounting to prudery. She also identifies herself with the great heroines of history, particularly with those who led a wild life before becoming heroines or nuns. She enjoys the mysticity of the religious life without any genuine religious feeling. She loves church for the sake of the flowers, and enjoys confession. On Sundays Chateaubriand's *Génie du Christianisme* is read aloud; Emma is moved by Chateaubriand's romantic melancholy, and develops a longing for tempestuous seas and ruins. In Chateaubriand's prose she is aware not of its artistry but of its power of awakening strong emotions; and she seeks these emotions for their own sake. Later, after the disappointment of her marriage and the first abortive love affair with Léon, we see that Emma's mind is either full of imagined satisfactions or (as Flaubert says) empty as a disused attic. The rhythm of her progressive disenchantment is constant: a mind full of vivid images and expectations, an attempt to find these imagined pleasures in life, disappointment and disillusion or frustration and deflation, a mind empty and cold, the refilling of the mind with new images. What Emma was incapable of learning, as Flaubert shows her to be, was the essential lesson which Flaubert believed himself to have learned; that the imagination can never find, in life, the equal of its imagining. As Baudelaire put it, in this world 'action is not the twin of dream'. Flaubert wrote in one of his letters that he had found a great truth: that wine has a taste unknown to those who drink it. 'Happiness lies in the idea, and nowhere else.' And this 'idea', which satisfies the imagination and brings repose to the mind, can only be achieved and fixed in literature, through style. 'From form the idea is born.'

The correspondences between Flaubert-Emma and Marcel the older-Marcel the younger are fairly easy to see. Marcel, until Bergotte reveals to him the meaning of style, makes mistakes about the enjoyment of literature comparable to Emma's, though never quite as crude. Like Flaubert, he came to see true satisfaction for his own spirit only in the spiritualization of sensuous experience through adequate expression, through style. True, this spiritualization is always associated with the pastness and recovery through memory of what is spiritualized; but he might have taken Flaubert's belief that 'wine has a taste unknown to those who drink it' and restated it in his own terms: perhaps 'life has pleasures unknown to those who live it'. True, between *Mme Bovary* and *A la recherche* comes the philosophy of Bergson, and Proust was prepared to suggest in *Le Temps retrouvé* that our spiritual awareness of life itself might be more acute and pleasurable if only the intelligence could be prevented from schematizing and desiccating the rich pulp of experience with which it has no business to concern itself; but the rich pulp itself, as Proust presents it, is almost purely sensuous. What has to be abstracted from experience to leave artistically transmutable 'impressions' is not only the utilitarian function of intelligence but the whole mechanism of moral responsibility—except the moral responsibility of the artist, engaged in the service of the amorally aesthetic. 'Aesthetic' here tends towards the narrowness of its etymology; and this is the sign of a spiritual limitation which deepens where it narrows, which produces a fictional world of unparalleled vividness from which so much of humanity is missing. In Flaubert and Proust we have writers assessing their experience in two modes, the lyrical and the pessimistically critical, and reconciling these two modes in novels reflecting the peculiar tensions, the irony, the sense of grotesque incompatibilities to which the two modes give rise.

The ideas contained in Marcel's first and other lessons, abstracted from Proust's narrative, appear nowadays to be platitudes; and in Proust's own day, if not quite the common currency they have become, they were already well handled and familiar to people who followed the aesthetic speculation of the century. But the narrative itself never loses its enchantment. Though its ostensible object is to lead us from observations about the pleasures of reading towards acceptance of conclusions to be clinched and interrelated in *Le Temps retrouvé*, when we return from a critical appraisal of Proust's ideas to the narrative (and others of the same kind) we return to the very essence of a pleasure; here, the pleasure of reading—at least a certain kind of pleasure we have all known in reading, and perhaps one which we may feel, with some regret, to be behind us. If we do, we shall find that Proust is still with us and has anticipated our judgment. For if Proust sometimes allows his desire to make art into an absolute to lead him into evasive tactics, he is at least honest when he does not evade. Art is made to the measure of mind, but Proust knows also that mind must be made to the measure of the kind of art it is to enjoy, and that if the immature mind misses the pleasures offered by, say, Stendhal, the mature mind misses the full glamour of the *Arabian Nights*. Part of Proust's ambition, in fact, is to create a work which will offer the mature mind the pleasures of both. But if Marcel read as he did, and aspired as he did to a future bright with the hope of what he read, it was, the narrator suggests, because he was not only less sophisticated but richer in potentialities than the narrator. There is in the narrator (and in Proust) a self who would give all the works of art in the world in exchange for these naïve dreams. At his moments of greatest frankness Proust is inclined to admit that art is not absolute, but only less relative than life, that the maturing of taste itself means loss as well as gain. Marcel will lose his capacity to enjoy Bergotte, will eventually fail to find in the enjoyment of any book the conviction that appears to be its own guarantee of value. His final word will be that books are only means of reading within oneself; that in certain states of the self there is nothing to read, and then books are useless; that there are certain parts of the self that no other man's book is adequate to make legible, and then one must write one's own; that, even then, there is in the true self an incommunicable residue. But this egotistic relativity, loyal to the detail of Proust's observation of his own experience, is constantly jarring with the wish to prove that art is absolute, that the 'ideas' which art reveals are not only intimately personal but also drawn from a common fund of universally valid 'ideas', and with the ambition to write the book which will be a universal instrument for all minds.

The first passage on reading in *Swann* leads almost immediately to Marcel's discovery of Bergotte and, through Bergotte, of the pleasure of style. Not until the end of his progress will Marcel realize that all other literary pleasures—including those of emotions and landscapes—depend on style; but already he realizes that through style literature becomes, instead of that pleasurable anticipation of what is to happen next which is, after all, too like the contingencies of living, a pleasure realized, held, and deepening rather than changing: a constant present. His notion of style is still insufficient; his mind separates, in Bergotte's works, the passages where 'style' is in the foreground from the narrative proper; he begins to prefer style to story and to mistake affectation for distinction. The style of Bergotte as Proust writes of it here is (as comparison with *Jean Santeuil* shows) compounded of the pseudo-archaic pomposity which Proust remembered enjoying in books which he later outgrew, like *Le Capitaine Fracasse*, and the more pretentious and sentimental phrases of Leconte de Lisle and Ruskin; it is the kind of style admiration for which makes literary-minded schoolboys speak as Bloch does and Proust once did. But the comparative crudity of the style which attracted the young Proust by its very extravagance is only forced on our attention when, with the aid of *Jean Santeuil* and some of Proust's early letters, we work back from *A la recherche* to the reality. Here we are given the boy's sense of adventure and discovery at the opening up of a fresh pleasure, intense enough to call for all the psalmody of heaven for its expression. Here, for the first time since the *madeleine* incident, the narrator speaks of a 'privileged moment' of plenitude and freedom. From that time onward Marcel feels every image of Bergotte to be a revelation; through Bergotte's style he feels for the first time the beauty of the things Bergotte writes of—forests, hail, *Notre-Dame de Paris*, *Athalie* and *Phèdre*. Some of Bergotte's 'revelations' correspond to Marcel's own 'discoveries'; occasionally he finds his own way of seeing things reflected in Bergotte's. In this Proust places the germ of Marcel's belief that he may be a born writer.

When, in *A l'ombre des jeunes filles*, Marcel meets Elstir, the latter's works take over the progressive education of Marcel in the Proustian aesthetic where Bergotte's left off. Albert Feuillerat has pointed out, after examining the proofs of the pre-war unprinted edition of this part of the book, that most of the account of the main Elstir episode was added as an afterthought; yet the ideas it conveys fit most wonderfully into the existing structure and improve both the pattern and the coherence.

Again they are selected for a special purpose. It is useless to expect from Proust a complete aesthetic of painting or even of Impressionism, which is the kind of painting Proust obviously has in mind here. He is concerned to stress his favourite points; to use some very particular observations on painting to support his view of literature and to suggest, at the same time, that his view of literature fits into a comprehensive view of all modes of art. In fact, this more lately elaborated passage supports the main conclusions of *Le Temps retrouvé* in greater detail than the passages on Vinteuil and music, many of which belong to the period when Proust's general plan was not clear enough to force its pattern on experience. In writing of Elstir's painting Proust knows more exactly what he is trying to demonstrate, and the evidence is marshalled and presented accordingly. Elstir is often said to be based on the French impressionist painters, and different critics favour different names; what is too often forgotten—though it has been clearly enough demonstrated—is that much of the material of this episode is worked up from suggestions Proust noted in his study of Ruskin. Behind his comments we can see Ruskin's writing on mediaeval architecture, Ruskin's remarks on Turner, and Turner's remarks as reported by Ruskin or by Robert de la Sizeranne who wrote a book introducing Ruskin's 'religion of beauty' to the French. But Proust has shorn away whatever his critical intelligence rejected, and cut the remainder to his own requirement.

The first lesson Elstir's work teaches (though again it is only the older Marcel who has absorbed it and can formulate it clearly) is that painting is not the imitation of nature but the *metamorphosis* of nature. This links with the lesson to be drawn from Bergotte's writing that literature is not a transcription but a transformation and reordering of life. Proust drives home his point by stating that Elstir's metamorphoses are analogous to the metaphors of writing; in his 'Port de Carquethuit' land is painted in terms of sea, sea in terms of land. Each element appears, in this novel perspective, to have invaded the other. The intelligence knows this interfusion of the elements to be false as representation, but in its misrepresentation lies its artistic effectiveness; its truth is of an unintellectual order; it is the truth of the impression. Not only is the impression *felt* as clarity and truth, distinct from the opaqueness and puzzlement of nature; it is also felt as *unity*, distinct from natural diversity and incoherence.

Again these ideas, abstracted from their concrete expression, are seen to be the common currency of Proust's contemporaries; easily translatable, for instance, into the main tenets of Baudelaire's theory of correspondences, though reticent about metaphysical sanctions. But, unlike Baudelaire and the Symbolists, Proust is always anxious to preserve the status of intelligence and its operations in art. So Elstir's work, like Proust's, is made to exhibit laws as well as register impressions; his paintings show intellectual discernment as well as irrational sensibility. Not only do they make use of novel perspective to suggest a fruitful misrepresentation of reality; they force the scrutinizing intellect to acknowledge that the *apparent* misrepresentation is such as might be *observed* in reality if the observer chose the same point of vantage as Elstir; and thus, concludes Proust, they enlighten the observer about the laws of perspective. Here, however, we see signs of the strain and special pleading which appear whenever Proust attempts to unite his irrational transcendentalism and his intellectualism in a single conception. For the objections to the 'metaphor' analogy which arise from the outset—for instance that no painting achieves its effect merely, if at all, by novel perspective, that the unity of a picture is brought about by modifications of reality belonging to the painter's idea, as much as to his vantage-point and that his idea, if it is subject to any laws, obeys laws of personal psychology rather than of perspective—objections to which the reader has perhaps paid little attention because they seemed irrelevant to Proust's demonstration, now oppose the very union of ideas which Proust is trying to bring about. Proust's novel exhibits 'laws' which our intelligence can abstract because Proust has consciously and intelligently worked them into it; but there are other great novels, and certainly great paintings, which do not. We have to read Proust's aesthetic not as disinterested speculation but as a compromise between disinterested speculation and the kind of artistic creation to which Proust found himself suited. Reduced to plain language, what Proust is saying is this: our most valuable spiritual experiences are the result of illusions about objective reality; art can do two things—record and perpetuate the valuable illusions and make clear the laws according to which such illusions arise in the mind. The potentiality of the spiritual experiences can only be situated in the self; yet this potentiality can only, it seems, be realized by projecting itself into objects outside the self which are then pursued with a passion which *appears* to be directed towards qualities in the object. The artist, instead of passionately *pursuing* the object, makes use of it, translates it into the language of his art—the style of painting or of literature—and thus captures and holds for ever the values of which, through the object, he has become aware.

Provided we allow Proust to limit our own speculation where he will and to select his evidence, we can appreciate the ingenuity with which he constructs his ideas into his system and, above all, the subtlety with which he presents them. For instance, Marcel comes across a portrait whose charm seems to be in its subject rather than in Elstir's 'metamorphosis' of it. Does this mean that things (or people) really can possess a charm other than that with which the artist's mind endows them? The suggestion conflicts with Proust's 'subjective idealism'. We like to believe that such things can exist, he says, because we are natural materialists. But reason combats the belief. There the subject is dropped, the problem left suspended. Later the solution is given, but we have to discover for ourselves that it *is* the solution, for it is propounded in another context. Marcel meets Mme Elstir. He sees a correspondence between her type of beauty and the style of Elstir's early paintings and realizes that Elstir has fallen in love with her because she represents a ready-made plastic expression, provided by nature, for the inner, personal ideals for which, until he met her, Elstir had had to discover his own plastic equivalents. There, then, is Proust's answer: nature sometimes provides the forms which our own ideals require for their expression. All this is an ingenious and fascinating way of making Marcel 'discover' that beauty is in the eye of the beholder and that the beauty of nature can be given a place, in Proust's aesthetic based on 'subjective idealism', which is properly subordinate to the beauty of art. Not only is the main passage on Elstir more closely adapted to the theoretical account of Marcel's own novel as it is given in *Le Temps retrouvé* than either the Bergotte or the Vinteuil material; it is also thinner in texture and more frankly expository. Proust is thinking more and feeling less. He is working on comparatively recent layers of feeling; the roots of his meditations on reading and music are growing strongly in *Jean Santeuil*, but painting as yet shows no signs of awakening a comparable interest.

There was in Proust a nostalgia for an absolute sanction for art, but his intellectual scepticism made it increasingly difficult for him to accept any philosophy which could provide it. His mind revolved like many nineteenth-century minds round the notion of transcendent 'ideas'. In *Jean Santeuil* the work of the novelist Traves expresses 'ideas' which 'no doubt had their home in heaven', ideas which find their way into his work in spite of the materialism and scepticism of Traves's consciously held philosophy. Jean Santeuil himself professes a kind of idealism which seems as eclectic and vague as Victor Cousin's but is obviously attached to experiences of Proust's which contained a true sense of devotion to overriding value. This same vaguely Platonic idealism permeates Proust's account of Vinteuil's music in *A la recherche*; like the literature of the nineteenth century according to Jean Santeuil, it is 'the expression of the mysterious truths which were for him the only truth'. To music, the most privileged and quintessential of all the arts according to the Symbolists and the philosophers dear to the Symbolists, Proust eventually accorded its privilege. But he found it more intractable than impressionist painting when he came to the task of presenting it in such a way that it could fit and support his explanation and justification of his own novel. So the older Proust gathered and concentrated the century's literary and philosophical account of music, which at one point he had been prepared to make his own, turned it into a concrete experience elaborated round a remembered experience of his own, the phrase of Saint-Saëns, and ascribed the philosophical commentary to Swann. 'Swann took musical themes to be real ideas, of another world, another order . . .' Proust could thus draw on whatever ideas he needed to characterize and reinforce the impression of the music, without intellectually committing himself to those ideas. The comments which he takes upon himself are more guarded: Swann, they suggest, was fundamentally right, but a little credulous in the detail of his account. He was, in fact, nearer the truth then than after his marriage, when music lost all value for him except as a sensation reminding him of his own past (this personal valuation of the mnemonic effect of music above its intrinsic expressive content, in *Jean Santeuil*, precedes the recognition of the Saint-Saëns fragment as at once recording and transcending the experience of Jean Santeuil's love for Françoise, the prototype of Swann's for Odette. Once more Proust is attributing to Swann's state of spiritual apathy an attitude he had himself adopted before he saw the light).

When, in *La Prisonnière*, Marcel himself takes over the commentary on Vinteuil's music, his emphasis is different. In *Swann*, Vinteuil is shown to have captured 'invisible ideas' which are the common spiritual heritage of humanity; in *La Prisonnière*, Vinteuil's ideas are 'irreducibly individual'; each artist's ideas come from a heaven, but each artist has his own heaven. It is useless, here, to look for a philosophy. Proust is simply stating his conviction of the transcendence, universality and uniqueness of the work of every great artist. These were things he had felt, and perceived more sharply when he read, in *Sesame and Lilies*, Ruskin's statement that beauty is an absolute existing outside individuals though perceived by each artist in an irreducibly individual form. He might equally have found the paradox implied in Baudelaire's *Salons*; Baudelaire, too, claimed that beauty is eternal and absolute but expressed by every age and country in its own way. Or he might have found the same idea in Hegel. Neglecting the background, we might judge that the first account of Vinteuil's music was Platonic, the second Bergsonian. In fact, the paradox itself is part of the thinking of the nineteenth century. The metaphysical trimmings are vehicles for the expression of aspects of the experience of works of art; the experiences are recognizable, but the comment takes us nowhere. Philosophically Proust, in the last event, is as puzzled as we are, though in his early volumes he has provided a wonderfully suggestive psychological account of the way in which the mysterious values to which Marcel is devoted first crystallized in the depths of his mind.

The philosophical discomfort is most apparent in *Le Temps retrouvé*; it is a carefully prepared explosion which sputters a little as if the powder were damp. The preparation for the final blaze is magnificent; Marcel touches the rock-bottom of disillusion and goes through a dark night of the soul, until a series of chance sensations open up visions of his own past which carry with them the sense of plenitude and freedom he had sometimes previously known but never explored or exploited. But after the first vigorous movement the rhythm flags. The long meditation on literature and art is sometimes confused in exposition, repetitive in its ideas and even in the very sentences which express them.

Some of this is accounted for by the lack of revision, since Proust died before he could prepare the end of his novel for the press. But there is another reason; the very difficulty of picking up all the statements about art made throughout the novel, accounting for every feature of the novel itself, relating these two sets of ideas, and showing how this complicated system was revealed to Marcel as the result of involuntary memory. Proust's efforts reveal the most astonishing intellectual resourcefulness, but he does not always play fairly. He shifts his viewpoint and changes his terms of reference without warning; there is a good deal of intellectual sleight-of-hand and more than a suspicion of sham profundity. The reader finds his feet caught in tangled coils of explanation when he should be flying; he may feel inclined to wish that Proust had been less anxious to explain. In matters aesthetic, Proust is always least authentic in abstraction; it is the impressions of real experience, or based on real experience, which are convincing and perennially fresh.

But even the intellectual conjuring tricks are stimulating and challenging, and they have been prompted by a genuine sense of correspondences which even Proust's intelligence has not been able to make manifest as clear intellectual relations; correspondences between that aspect of the expressive power of painting which Impressionism isolated and concentrated and that aspect of the expressive power of language which Symbolism isolated and concentrated; correspondences between language, so specialized, and music; correspondences between the kind of lyricism which Symbolism selected from the romantic range and the kind Proust experienced through involuntary memory; the importance to this specialized symbolist language of the fusion metaphor. All these offer problems enough; but to those problems which belong to the fashionable speculation of his age Proust added others. Where Mallarmé, for instance, was content to depreciate all poetry which did not fit his own aesthetic as diluted and debased, Proust, infinitely more catholic in his appreciation of literature than most of his contemporaries, was looking for an aesthetic which could comprehend Classicism as well as Romanticism, memoirs as well as poetry. The range of his speculation is such that he may be forgiven some confusion. It is as well to recognize that any full account of the power of literature would have to take note of factors to which he, as well as his contemporaries, was blind; but he had the courage and independence, in an age of literature almost entirely devoted to the exploration of feeling and the exercise of imaginative freedom, to recognize that intellectual power is an asset even for the artist, and that we ought to be able to look to art for understanding as well as rapture.

VII

Free Fantasia

Proust's account of Marcel's vocation as the expression of ideals realized in impressions and of ideas reflecting the understanding of laws governing human behaviour left him free to construct a fiction which is not only the creation of a subjectivity but the creation and explanation of the world in which that subjectivity exists. Proust's theory was based on aesthetic ideas produced by the romantic tradition to account for and assure the philosophical prestige of the kind of lyrical ecstasy which Baudelaire called 'rapture of the soul'. Baudelaire felt something of the mystery and wonderment which he associated with the supernatural when he read Balzac's novels as well as when he read the more romantic poems of Gautier, and thought of both writers as *voyants*, as revealers of a transcendent world. Flaubert, concerned with his own purely literary, metaphysically agnostic kind of transcendence, proclaimed that happiness lay in the 'idea' of satisfactions rather than in the achievement of satisfactions in experience, that the 'idea' was to be realized by literary style, and that ideally he would like to write a novel which had no plot and no characters, nothing but style. But he admitted that this kind of 'pure' novel was a chimera, just as Proust had to admit his kind of 'pure' novel was a chimera. If we think of the larger conception of style, the style of which plot, character, and style in the narrower sense are all part, then the style of *Madame Bovary* is the equivalent of an 'idea': Flaubert has achieved a means of holding certain regions of experience in the mind in a satisfactory way. This notion of 'style' however is applicable to any work of art, irrespective of the importance given to 'style' in the narrower sense, the sense in which we say that Gide is a stylist, or that Flaubert took pains over his style which Balzac did not. Running through the century, we find the concern with style in the narrower sense from a moment marked approximately by Hugo's essay proclaiming that 'the future belongs to style'; and within this current of speculation on style we find a continuing preoccupation with metaphor (not restricted to France, and coeval with Romanticism in all its manifestations throughout Europe) and with the belief that the experience of the transcendental in literature arises from the fusion, in metaphor, of logically disparate elements; that the Idea arises from the imaginative fusion of ideas which, naturally, are related in such a way that reason is incapable of apprehending the significance of that relation. Baudelaire, whose theory of correspondences centres on such a

66

notion of the metaphor, could admit Balzac to the company of *voyants* unreflectingly. Reason, for him, always went down in matters artistic before intuition. He had little tendency to dilate on technical problems, and little occasion to dwell on problems specific to the novel. He was not hag-ridden by the kind of scepticism which made Proust test the ideas that won his emotional assent against his own intelligence, and made him finally condemn Ruskin for intellectual dishonesty. Proust must both have felt and partly understood what linked his own sensibility with Baudelaire's, Emerson's, Ruskin's and others like them; he must have looked in the philosophers he read (or read about) for a more complete theory, and found many variations or alternatives all centred on oneirism and transcendence, the subconscious, the subrational, dream, instinct, intuition; and states of consciousness which could be called beauty, a consciousness of plenitude, freedom and devotion. Proust seems to have accepted, from all sides, observations of detail which fitted his own experience, but rejected all systems with sceptical irony. His own attempt at an aesthetic, richly suggestive and stimulating in the detail of its own observations, is disappointing as a system; most suggestive in the course of the novel where it applies itself to a number of independent subjects, most disappointing in *Le Temps retrouvé* where all the fragments of explanation ought to be brought together into a system to provide the key to Marcel's vocation. Proust had set himself an enormous problem. He had to adapt the interrelated ideas of Baudelaire, Emerson, Ruskin and so on to his own case, which meant refusing a too-easy reliance on the idea of supernatural revelation, attempting to give a 'rational' explanation without falling back on religion and an after-life (here Bergson, with his importation of the eternal within time, within the limits of human life, had hints to offer), bringing 'memory' and not 'vision' into the centre of the picture, and adapting to prose style a theory of metaphor first applied to poetry. Proust had also to extend the symbolist aesthetic to cover aspects of his work which had manifestly nothing to do with dreams, visions and revelations, and he could do it only by grafting on to it a quite distinct and even alien claim for the artistic importance of intellectual understanding.

This 'aesthetic' is a kind of trick. But having performed it tolerably, Proust was free to include in his novel the most varied presentations of experience and attitudes to experience. When the foundations of the book's structure had been laid, and the two pillars of the first and last volumes constructed, Proust was left with a good deal of liberty in the elaboration of the superstructure; whatever he found it interesting to add could be tied in to the relevant supports, or even carried as inessential ornament on the components which did carry the architectural stresses.

Proust made full use of this freedom. The progress from the

formlessness of *Jean Santeuil* to the organic structure of *A la recherche* involved first selection and pruning of the autobiographical material until the main stems were growing in the right direction. Marcel's personality was to be shown rooted in childhood impressions, and these impressions had to be concentrated, reinforced, stylized; the movements of the imagination had to be centred in dominant symbols. Fantasy had to be disciplined within the bounds of the demonstration. The stages of Marcel's spiritual growth had to be clearly marked, the climax carefully prepared. But once this discipline was accomplished, Proust was free to embroider at will, and he embroidered so lavishly that his plan was all but obscured for any but his most attentive readers. During the war years, when the publication of the book was held up, the matter proliferated steadily, as it had done from the moment of its planning, but now there was no printer to arrest the process.

In *Le Temps retrouvé*, at a moment when Proust is least philosophical, least bound by the need to fit his comment on his own work into a metaphysical demonstration, he compares his book to a cathedral, a frock pinned together piece by piece, and one of Françoise's best dishes, the *boeuf mode* so much appreciated by Norpois. All those images are suggestive and revealing. The book is planned as a cathedral must be planned, planned as a shrine to the religion of art, as a monument piled up by the past and a means of recovery of the past's spirituality. But it was not built as a cathedral must be built, stone on stone, it was put together as a designer puts together a frock, pinning his ornaments on the first drape and standing back to look at the effect. And the parts fitted into the whole were chosen as the best of their kind. Just as Françoise chose the best meat for her *boeuf mode*, Proust chose the best and most interesting experiences of a rich if inwardly bitter life. Yet something must be added to these images to complete the picture. As Proust wrote and added he had less and less of rich and strange impressions to draw on and more and more of shrewd, detached observation. He could remake the magic of Combray, with a great creative effort, by supplementing memory and imagination with Gaston Bonnier' *Flora*; he could ask his women friends to bring out their old hats and frocks to help out remembered atmospheres with descriptive fact; but much more easily could he move on occasions from his cork-lined room into the still active outside world and, turning his developed and specialized vision on to the social antics from which he had now withdrawn, add incident after incident, fresco after fresco, to the human comedy whose vanity points up the drama and reward of artistic vocation. And so, more and more, the aspects of the book which are tied into the fundamental structure by the thinnest stays, or resting merely on its surface, were developed in their own right, for their own intrinsic interest. In a narrative stretched over half a century half a volume out of fifteen is devoted to a single dinner-party

68

From the beginning, scenes from the human comedy are slipped into passages whose chief concern is the life of Marcel's imagination. Characters slip from the background to the foreground and begin to exist in their own right: Aunt Léonie, as a variation on the perennial theme of the hypochondriac; Françoise who, like the figures carved on the porch of Saint-André-des-Champs which bring her to Marcel's mind, in her mixture of superstition and shrewdness, cruelty and devotion, snobbery and independence sums up virtues, failings and oddities which Proust felt to be characteristic of the uneducated servant class in the France of his time; Legrandin, the first of the lay figures which Proust is to use to record his anatomy of snobbery. The Swann love story brings in Mme Verdurin. She is multipurposed: an important agent in the narrative of Swann's love for Odette and Charlus's for Marcel; an illustration of the transformation of society, since she is to expose the sham of her own inverted snobbery by marrying the Prince de Guermantes; but also a great if exaggeratedly caricatured comic figure. In her salon are set the first of the elaborate conversation pieces which, as Mansfield has pointed out, can be detached as self-sufficient comic interludes, and from which, as Fernandez writes, the narrator seems to be as detached as if he were a folklore expert or a student of dialects playing the records he had collected of the speech habits of an alien people.

The introduction of the 'little phrase' of Vinteuil's sonata, itself integral to the 'vocation theme', is the pretext for one of the great set-pieces, Mme de St. Euverte's reception. It is interesting here that Swann is said to be able to see the pretentious elegance of this particular stratum of the Faubourg Saint-Germain because he has become detached from it by his devotion to Odette and returns to it with eyes cleared of the film of long habit and unquestioning acceptance. He returns to it, in fact, like Proust emerging from his retreat. And Proust uses the opportunity to exercise his talent for transforming human beings into specimens, to offer the reader a peep at his human zoo. Metaphor, here, is abundant; not the fusion metaphors of the romantic tradition but metaphors underlining the grotesque disparity between the people and the things they recall to Proust's mind. Footmen and guests are thrust out of their normal context and placed in the contexts of animal nature or Renaissance painting, and the mockery spills over a little on to the inflated humanism of the paintings referred to. The comic climax is achieved when M. de Palancy, whose name constantly calls out fishlike imagery, becomes a carp, and his monocle a symbolic fragment of his aquarium.

In *A l'ombre des jeunes filles* we are carried into a new complex of spiritual and erotic associations, parallel with and to some extent growing out of the earlier Combray pattern. Instead of the hawthorns, Combray church, Bergotte and Gilberte, we have the sea, Balbec church, Elstir and Albertine. And, as previously, the novel's rhythm proceeds by a complicated process of overlapping. The Albertine story is left in suspense while the Guermantes story is picked up again, for at Balbec Marcel meets Oriane's nephew, Robert de Saint-Loup, and her brother-in-law, Palamède, Baron de Charlus. From the Faubourg Saint-Germain we move to Sodom and Gomorrha, the underworld of sexual perversion in which all classes are united by their senses and instincts. Then the Albertine story is resumed.

In the meantime, the procession of characters in the human comedy continues.

With *A l'ombre des jeunes filles* comes the Baron de Norpois, who at one time had made one character with Charlus, now separated off as the type of the long-winded, cliché-ridden diplomat with no qualification but the hidebound conviction which hides his spiritual obtuseness and timidity; Mme de Villeparisis, a particularly interesting social type because, as a *déclassée*, she cuts across the normal stratification; the Bloch family, another collection of caricatures comparable to the *clan Verdurin*. But it is in the middle section of the novel—*Le côté de Guermantes* and *Sodome et Gomorrhe*—that the human comedy comes to and stays in the foreground. The shattering of Marcel's dream of the name 'Guermantes' is effectively dealt with in comparatively little space; through it, and constant references to Combray, the earlier themes of the novel are kept in mind. There is a long section on Marcel's visit to Doncières, where Saint-Loup is garrisoned. No doubt this originated in a cherished memory of Proust's real life, since there is a very long section in *Jean Santeuil* about Jean's stay with Henri de Réveillon in similar circumstances. But here, as elsewhere, the comparison of *Jean Santeuil* with *A la recherche* shows the degree of imaginative transmutation undergone by the autobiographical material. The story of Marcel's ephemeral and absurd passion for Oriane de Guermantes is told, and that of Saint-Loup's for Rachel (which illustrates the same Proustian 'laws' of love as Swann's and Marcel's) is begun. But more and more space is given to the broad frescoes, the satirical observation of character and manners, the impact of the Dreyfus affair on individuals and groups.

Then Palamède de Charlus advances to the centre of the stage, to dominate, as a character, the whole book. He is the personification of arrogance—arrogance of the kind Marcel's grandfather found so fascinating in Saint-Simon's story of the commoner who, 'through ignorance or as a try-on', offered his hand to his sons. He is, further, a sometimes comic and eventually nightmarish projection of the frightening and shameful perversion which Proust knew within himself. But he is also a sensitive and vulnerable creature, and the arrogance itself gives the measure of his humiliation at the hands of Mme Verdurin and of his abjection when he last appears as a decrepit and dependent old man. He is grandiose, grotesque and infinitely pathetic. Of all the characters Proust used to put his own vices at a distance and establish a tenable attitude towards them, Charlus is the richest and most subtly drawn.

To the successive subjective 'worlds' of Marcel's imagination are added, then, the objective 'worlds' or social groups into which human beings become organized, the astronomical system of which Marcel, like a social Newton, has 'discovered' the laws of motion. Here, as in the subjective scheme, Proust's observations have been stylized and, as far as possible, arranged in a system; again the creative process is marked by three stages: observation, abstraction of general principles, the imaginative re-creation, round these abstract principles, of human reality. But here, far more than in the case of Marcel's subjective life, one is aware that the re-created reality is not quite human. The account is given not by a humanist but by a naturalist, and by a naturalist whose field of speculation and categories of systematization are limited by his personal obsessions. Like Descartes' whirlwinds, Proust's social astronomy is impressive but obviously false; its correspondence with our own experience is close enough to allow us to admire the mental powers which have exercised themselves in the perfection of its internal coherence, but not close enough to convince us that its coherence is adequate to the complexity of the world in which we are involved. Proust's world is not quite our world, but it is imaginatively authentic. When Marcel reduces his haloes to ideas, these ideas are still part of Proust's imaginative construction. They are sufficiently based on lucid observation to help us to order and clarify our own experience of ourselves and others; but they need supplementation to become fully human. In the last event Proust's world is arranged in superficial and delightful pattern rather than penetrated in tragic depth.

Marcel the child sees two social spheres outside his own— Swann's and Oriane's; about these and his own he entertains illusions, among them being the belief that the two unknowns are intrinsically superior. Having penetrated their mystery he can be 'objective' about all three. The superiority of the Guermantes' world, its highest poetry, he annexes to his own idealism; there remains a lower poetry, an irreducible individuality, a fascination exerted by the Guermantes in their own right. The halo proper belongs elsewhere, but there remains the harder, colder radiation of *l'esprit des Guermantes*. What Proust takes most pleasure in making plain, however, is the system of laws which binds all three social worlds together, and within them smaller worlds, and, within these, individuals. Marcel's subjective 'worlds' were individual and distinct, but linked by the same underlying patterns. The same is true of social groups.

Mme Brée has remarked that the shadow of Louis XIV and Saint-Simon helps to pattern Proust's world. There are a number of 'courts' gravitating about their sovereigns—the Faubourg Saint-Germain round Charlus (more truly, perhaps, round the Guermantes as a family), Eulalie and Françoise round Aunt

Léonie, the lower servants round Françoise, the staff of the Grand Hotel at Balbec round the manager. We can add the 'little clan' formed round Mme Verdurin. Each court has its own ritual and its own mechanisms for the preservation of self-esteem. Each member has to put on the appropriate mask and dance the ritual dance; to fail to conform is to risk extrusion, as Swann and Charlus are extruded by Mme Verdurin. There is a hierarchy of courts; one of the conventions of each is its exclusiveness—real when directed downwards, sham as regards those above. The generality of these principles is demonstrated, and all societies shorn of their pretensions, by their application to the 'Marquise' who looks after the public lavatories in the Champs-Elysées; for she also has her standards, and is particular about whom she admits.

We, endowed with the narrator's omniscience, are pleasured with the spectacle of all these people shut within their ignorance and unconscious of it. We know that they are moved by the same futile motives as the 'Marquise', and they do not. We see when they are behaving incongruously, unaware of the ritual which is expected of them, of the essential differences between their own and that of other groups. We hear them repeating in all seriousness the enormities which they are made to utter by their ignorance, or their total inability, under the stress of unconscious inhibitions, to allow themselves to see the truth. Nobody can truly know anybody else—that is a fundamental proposition of Proust's 'subjective idealism'; but to this philosophical veto is added, in the general run of humanity, a positive unwillingness to know what *can* be known. The humour of this spectacle of human beings enclosed within less-than-human limitations—blindness, stupidity, ignorance, prejudice, vice— is in the comic tradition. But compare it with Molière's, where there is the assumption of a norm from which the inhumanity is seen as a deviation; here there is no norm except the figure of the artist, no remedy except withdrawal into disinterested contemplation, composed of sensuous lyricism, the bitter-sweet of understanding, and (though the aesthetic theory makes no mention of this) a humour sometimes bordering on cruel contempt.

Whatever the character of the subject-matter, Proust the narrator is continually present as the presiding intelligence. Even when Marcel is not present—as when Swann's story is being told and Marcel has not been born, or when Marcel effaces himself behind the narrative of scenes in which he is not personally concerned—the narrator, Proust, the older Marcel of the fiction, is passing the substance of his sensibility and imagination through the filter and mould of his intelligence. Even in passages which the theory of involuntary memory seems most satisfactorily to account for, those passages of impressions which seem most truly 'outside time'—almost the whole account of Combray, in which happenings are dissolved in states, (in particular, the account of the two 'ways'), the less sustained notations of the very 'feel' of Balbec and the sunlit sea, the increasingly fugitive statements of climate and atmosphere—the narrator is there not only to create the past but to point, comment, deprecate, patronize and lighten with irony and humour. What varies is the relation between the delight of what is felt to have been (or what is now projected into) the past, and the delight in the narrator's manner of presentation, between sensibility and shrewdness, tenderness and malice, compassion and humour. Too often Marcel has the lion's share of the first of these pairs of terms, and the rest of the world is the victim of the second; though Marcel, too, in his young and naïve days, comes in for his share of mockery. But even when Proust is living in Marcel's lost paradises, his joy is as much in the present act of creating with words as in the delight of what is in part recovered and in part created. With him, the rapture of the soul never means the rape of the intelligence. Like others of his contemporaries, he belongs to the latter stage of a long romantic tradition, where one part of that tradition sweeps on into the convulsions of Surrealism, and another sweeps back towards the perennial virtues of the French mind—lucidity, delicacy and sureness of touch.

In respect of his detachment as a writer from what he is writing about, even when what he is writing about is himself, Proust may be compared to Lautréamont. Each, in his time, had nourished his imagination on books rather than on active experience and had sensed reverberations from romantic literature to his own deep-lying but not suppressed, controlled, or organized unconscious movements. To what extent played a part in Lautréamont's use of the shadier romantic themes we can only speculate, and it would be unprofitable to compare his exploration or exploitation of the oneiric with Proust's. But each, in his way, was consciously using his awareness of oneiric experience, and, in the work of each, part of the individuality of the work and the peculiarity of its pleasure (keeping the necessary proportions between a minor and a major writer) comes from the parallel awareness of oneiric power and intelligence. It is worth while pressing the point a little further, for the suggestion that the act of creating any considerable literary work can be lacking in conscious control and criticism is likely nowadays to offend. The point is that whereas, when the critic is studying the creative process of, say, Baudelaire or even Rimbaud, he may maintain that the choice of the means of expression is always a consciously critical act, he must admit that the reader's awareness of the work itself may involve a greater or less degree of self-awareness with respect to the experience proposed. Baudelaire and Rimbaud propose a surrender to the incantatory power of the style and the affective impact of the images, and one aspect of the development of Symbolism was the sacrifice of logical and (to some extent) syntactical coherence to 'supralogic'. Proust and Lautréamont both have a classical respect for the logic of language.

Only through long acquaintance with the work is the subtlety of Proust's style, and the attitudes it communicates, apparent. One critic will deprecate for its pre-Raphaelite affectations and preciosity a passage in which another will see a redeeming irony; one will point to the pathos of an event or character which to another seems comic. In general (and one must make this limitation because there are occasions when technique becomes empty mannerism) the subtlety bears a direct relation to the syntactical complication. If Proust never depends in true symbolist fashion on the supralogical clash of impression-laden images, the effect of his complicated constructions is that the images strike first and the precise relations between the images emerge afterwards, and only as these relations are taken by the mind do the exactly relevant impressions from the images oust the irrelevant. The proper appreciation of Proust's attitude to what he is putting before the reader depends not only on a minutely adjusted awareness of local style but on bringing to bear on particular instances impressions derived from the book as a whole, on the cross-reference of attitudes. Even then, there is sometimes an ambiguity of feeling which turns his prose into shot silk traversed by change. Less, however, than the obtuseness of some of his commentators would give one to suppose. Let us look at an instance of how a translator has failed to take Proust's mood.

In the main passage on the hawthorns, there is a patronizing reference to nature to which we referred earlier. Here is the original text, with the operative words in italics:

> Et certes, je l'avais tout de suite senti, comme devant les épines blanches mais avec plus d'émerveillement, que ce n'était pas facticement, par un artifice de fabrication humaine, qu'était traduite l'intention de festivité dans les fleurs, mais que c'était la nature qui, spontanément, l'avait exprimée avec la *naïveté d'une commerçante de village* travaillant pour un reposoir, en *surchargeant* l'arbuste de ces rosettes d'un *ton trop tendre* et d'un *pompadour provincial*.

The mood here is complicated. There is tenderness as well as patronage, of the sort which the older Marcel extends to his earlier self and to the past in which the other self lived. Scott-Moncrieff, unable no doubt to admit emotions which seemed irrelevant to the context, simplified the attitude in his translation:

> And, indeed, I had felt at once, as I had felt before the white blossom, but now still more marvelling, that it was in no artificial manner, by no device of human construction, that the festal intention of these flowers was revealed, but that it was Nature herself who had spontaneously expressed it (with the simplicity of a woman from a village shop, labouring at the decoration of a street altar for some procession) by burying the bush in these little rosettes, almost too ravishing in colour, this rustic 'pompadour'.

'Simplicity' distorts 'naïveté', 'burying' attenuates 'surchargeant', 'little rosettes' is gratuitous, 'ravishing', though not too far from the dictionary meaning of 'tendre', substitutes new overtones to those given to the word here by its context.

Proust's method of writing, then, bears out his theory to the extent that impressionism is served by intelligence in the shaping of its 'spiritual equivalent'. What the theory does not admit is that to the 'spiritual equivalent' of past impressions is added a present attitude.

Fernandez, in his own summing-up of Proust's qualities, quotes a passage written by Jacques Rivière on the relaunching of the *Nouvelle revue française* in 1919, which looks forward to a new phase of literature applying a lucid intelligence to the inventory of the sensations and emotions brought into literature by Romanticism and Symbolism. No author has done more to bring about that dream than Proust. His book is a philosophic mystery—some have called it a 'metaphysical detective story'—to which the key is provided in the finale. The creation of the 'vision' is the work of the imagination, but the elaboration of the structure on which it is created is the work of a keen and powerful intelligence analyzing and synthesizing in the service of imagination, working on an amazingly wide culture apprehended by a fine sensibility and recorded by a quite exceptional memory biased, like Stendhal's and Fromentin's, though less exclusively, towards impressions rather than facts. What gives the mystery and the key their authenticity, the validity which suspends disbelief at least to the extent of providing aesthetic satisfaction, is, besides their internal aesthetic coherence, their close correspondence with those of the nineteenth-century attitudes to art to which we are now inclined to attach most value. *A la recherche* is a human comedy, but it is also the Divine Comedy of the religion of art; it is the bodying forth in an imaginatively created world of the aesthetic idealism underlying romantic and symbolist literature, as Dante's poem is the bodying forth of the abstractions of Aquinas, the breath of life coming from a lyrical tradition both sensuous and mystical.

Paradoxically, perhaps, Proust's originality depends in part upon his own catholicity and powers of absorption, upon the richness and variety of the substance he drew from others. But it also depends on his powers of digesting and transmuting. When he accepted and absorbed ideas, it was because he had lived the experience to which the ideas referred, or could refer it to his own and translate it into his own terms. We mentioned earlier that in *Jean Santeuil* Proust notes an idea which much preoccupied Baudelaire and other students of the imagination —that of the analogies and distinctions between the ecstasies of art and drugs. In *A la recherche*, the idea is translated into the terms of Proust's subjective idealism and presented in concrete images when Marcel drinks too much in the restaurant at Rivebelle; alcohol provides him with a precarious and caricatural correspondence of the sense of plenitude and freedom which his art is to create and fix. Similarly, the banal romantic obsession with the gulf between imagination and reality is turned into specific experiences, the most strikingly vivid of which are the account of the pleasures of reading and the scene where Marcel stands nonplussed before the distressing solidity of the figures carved on the façade of Balbec church, reflecting that he could write his name on the statue of the Virgin already desecrated by having an existence in spatially extended—and limited—matter. The passage from general ideas to concrete realizations of the corresponding experience allowed innumerable variations on the same theme.

Nor are the pleasures of the 'metaphysical detective novel' to be despised. Clues are planted everywhere like needles in a haystack, threaded and interconnecting. When we read the book first it is often difficult to put our hand on the clue we need; but continually, as we go back over supposedly familiar passages, new clues unexpectedly prick our attention and add their quota to the intricate pattern.

There are passages which are tedious; there is a good deal of repetition. But Proust is so successful a spellbinder that even tedium is felt rather as the willing wait for the next confidently expected stretch of amusement or delight. Even when we are slightly bored, we are still living in another world, a world commanded by the steady, meticulous, apparently disinterested voice of the narrator, so finally convinced of the ultimate importance even of his own platitudes that the reader does not recognize their familiarity until he has disentangled an abstract idea or general observation from the sinuous rills of a style which keeps the garden bright even when it is enfolding no sunny spots of greenery. At his artistically feeblest, Proust is a great conversationalist of whom we are willing to miss very little; even a long discourse on the art of warfare, a subject on which we can hardly expect Proust to provide anything but the most bookish information, may yield a gem or two of comment, some outside slant on the world to which not only Saint-Loup belongs but General Froberville with his monocle fixed in his eye like a shining shell fragment.

And so, unless we dislike Proust and are looking for a stick to beat him with, we do not ask too pertinaciously, as we read, to what purpose we are being told what Proust is telling us. The plan of the book is there, and can be exhibited to refute the critics who said that Proust's work is amorphous; but the amount of work which must go to its exhibition gives some point to the criticism. If Proust found it difficult to leave anything out which he could possibly fit in, it is because of his unbounded curiosity and interest. Like Marcel's grandmother, Proust talks of the objects of his interest 'with that detached, smiling, almost sympathetic benevolence with which we reward the object of our disinterested observation for the pleasure which it procures us'.

If his undoubted pessimism about human relations is so rarely depressing, it is because he communicates, at least to the sympathetic reader, his delight at finding people out, at finding life out, his exhilaration at 'blowing the gaff', to borrow Professor Empson's name for a stock literary process. Such determined deflation relieves, for us, the strain of maintaining our own optimism, like Voltaire's 'bon père de famille est capable de tout'.

Too often, in romantic writing, we find such stock literary processes isolated and exalted into philosophies. This marks a disequilibrium which has its serious implications in so far as it reflects the disequilibrium of our culture; but when the irony and humour go out of such attitudes they can become wearisome personal complaints, and often the depression and discouragement they represent is offset only, apart from a delight in destruction grown lyrical, by the sense of value and purpose represented by the form in which the complaint is cast. Even the most pessimistic work of art, as Valéry observes somewhere, is never merely depressing; it contains its own dose of exhilaration. In nineteenth-century writing about the status of literature, the exalting of art is often balanced by the disparagement of life; but never, before Proust, has the disparagement of life been so successfully shouted down within the work of art itself, by the triumphant cry of purpose achieved, of destiny worked out in the teeth of despair and to the point of death. *A la recherche* does not contain the whole truth about human life, but it does contain some essential truth about Proust's.

In part it is false even to Proust's, however. Not simply because Marcel is a simplified and idealized Proust, the simplification and idealization being part of the creative effort by which Proust finally achieved his purpose, part of the imaginative rectification of his world. This kind of insincerity can sometimes be exacted by some greater consideration of artistic sincerity. Rather because in the account of Marcel's success the given is emphasized at the expense of the won, revelation at the expense of effort. It has often been admitted that the novel shows no awareness of any morality but that of the creative artist; what it does not sufficiently bring out within itself is the importance, even for the artist—and particularly for Proust—of an effort which is itself fundamentally moral. It is nearer, in feeling, to a fairy tale for very sophisticated adults than to a mature and tragic awareness of human responsibility.

One can see what Bergson meant when he said that *A la recherche du temps perdu* fails to exalt and brace the spirit. One can see the point, too, of the adverse English criticisms collected together by Floris Delattre. D. H. Lawrence said that Proust's novel was made of water-jelly. George Moore said Proust reminded him of a man trying to plough a field with knitting-needles. Desmond McCarthy said he was completely and extravagantly romantic, a kind of Lady of Shalott who never lifts his eyes from his magic mirror. F. L. Lucas called his philosophy 'a muddled idealism' and the author a cross between Mephistopheles and Machiavelli. Cyril Connolly said that in Proust the terror of having to make a decision and the fear of leaving something out have put on the masks of love and truth. To all of these criticisms Proust is vulnerable. He tried to stretch an inadequate philosophy too far. He had the good sense to avoid the more extravagant of the conclusions which his over-simple idealism implied, as when, having been led to the point of making the notion of German war guilt a nationally subjective valuation on the part of the French, he saw the moral nihilism which such a theory of valuation implied, and stopped short. There were problems of and about human life which Proust never touched on because they were not his, and some of these omissions bear on his treatment of the problems which he felt to be peculiarly his. It has been said that he de-dramatizes society and de-dramatizes love. It has also been said that his very originality and, partly, merit, lie in having de-dramatized the French novel, casting off from it the shackles put on it by the prestige of classical tragedy and making it free of its own dimension, which is feeling rather than deeds. Yet it is difficult to see how any account of feeling can be complete without taking account of such feelings as are concerned with the interchange in reality, meaning here the sphere of behaviour as distinct from the sphere of subjective flux, between the self and the non-self. It is one of the limitations of Proust's gifts that he cannot take seriously any passion which is not the pursuit of a state of mind; his pathological self-reference has enriched his presentation of life in some directions and impoverished it in others.

But to condemn a work because it fails in some particular respect is to fail to heed the warning of artists as different as Hugo and Mallarmé, who both pointed to the critical error which consists of expecting fruit from a flowering tree—or, to adapt the image, potatoes from a peach. Rebecca West once compared *A la recherche du temps perdu* to a velvet-gloved hand stretched out to grasp a peach, and contrasted its leisurely movement with the convulsive clutch of James Joyce in *Ulysses*. It is useless to ask Proust for the sense of discovering or recovering our own inner energies and convictions which Dostoevsky and Melville can awaken; Proust's spirit is not the breath of life itself, but a refinement and enrichment of life. A peach, perhaps even a little soft in places, but carrying no threat to sound digestions. The book carries its own antidote; its range of sensation is from the sensuality of Petronius to the devoted sensuousness of Keats.

BIOGRAPHICAL NOTE

1871 (10th July) Proust born at Auteuil, near Paris.

1880   First attack of asthma. According to Léon Pierre-Quint, Proust was no longer able to spend his summer holidays in the country, and went instead to the sea.

1887–1888 Proust contributes articles to reviews founded and edited by his schoolfellows at the Lycée Condorcet.

1889   Military service with the 76th Infantry Regiment at Orléans.

1892   Contributes society notes and book reviews to *Le Banquet,* a review founded by the Lycée Condorcet group.

1893   Meets the Comte Robert de Montesquiou-Fezensac.

1894   Proust obtains an unpaid post as assistant at the Mazarine Library, but does not assume his duties.

1895–1900 (about) At work on a long novel, eventually abandoned (posthumously published as *Jean Santeuil*).

1900   Begins serious study and translation of Ruskin.

1903   Death of Proust's father.

1905   Death of his mother.

1906(?)   Proust begins to write the novel which will eventually become *A la recherche du temps perdu.*
Leaves his parents' house and moves to 102, Boulevard Haussmann. Lives in increasing solitude in his cork-lined bedroom.

1908–1910 Turns aside from novel to write a critical study of Sainte-Beuve (posthumously published as *Contre Sainte-Beuve*). This work leads to a further exploration of memories of his own past, and to the development of themes and narratives later to be incorporated in *A la recherche du temps perdu.*

1911   First 700 pages ready for printing. Proust in search of a publisher. *N.R.F.* (advised by André Gide) rejects the manuscript, but takes over publication from Grasset after the appearance of the first volume.

1913–1922 Proust continues to revise and expand the later parts of his novel as the earlier parts are published.

1922 (18th November) Proust dies, with the last five volumes still unpublished.

BIBLIOGRAPHICAL NOTE

WORKS

1896   *Portraits de peintres*
        Les Plaisirs et les jours

1904   *La Bible d'Amiens* (Ruskin). Translation, preface and notes by Prous

1906   *Sésame et les lys* (Ruskin). Translation, preface and notes by Proust

1913   *Du côté de chez Swann*

1919   *A l'ombre des jeunes filles en fleurs*
        Pastiches et mélanges

1920–27 Remaining volumes of *A la recherche*

1927   *Chroniques*

1952   *Jean Santeuil*

1954   *Contre Sainte-Beuve*

WORKS AVAILABLE IN ENGLISH TRANSLATION

1922–31 *Remembrance of Things Past*. Translated by C. K. Scott-Moncrieff (*Swann's Way* to *The Sweet Cheat Gone*) and Stephen Hudson (*Time Regained*)

1941   Uniform Edition

1948   *Marcel Proust: A Selection from His Miscellaneous Writings*. Translated by Gerard Hopkins

1950   *Letters of Marcel Proust*, Selected, edited and translated by Mina Curtiss

1955   *Jean Santeuil*. Translated by Gerard Hopkins
        In preparation *Contre Sainte-Beuve*. Translated by Sylvia Townsend Warner

SOME WORKS ON PROUST IN ENGLISH

1940   Derrick Leon, *Introduction to Proust*

1948   Harold March, *The Two Worlds of Marcel Proust*

1949   F. C. Green, *The Mind of Proust*

1950   André Maurois, *The Quest for Proust*. Translated by Gerard Hopkins

1950   Martin Turnell, *The French Novel*

1952   P. A. Spalding, *A Reader's Handbook to Proust*
        In preparation Germaine Brée, *Marcel Proust and the Deliverance from Time*